CONTINUUM STUDIES IN PASTORAL CARE AND PERSONAL
AND SOCIAL EDUCATION

MEDITATION IN SCHOOLS

)F

Related titles:

Ron Best (ed.): *Education, Spirituality and the Whole Child*

Ron Best (ed.): *Education for Spiritual, Moral, Social and Cultural Development*

Ron Best, Peter Lang and Anna Lichtenberg (eds): *Caring for Children: International Perspectives on Pastoral Care and PSE*

Ron Best, Peter Lang, Caroline Lodge and Chris Watkins (eds): *Pastoral Care and PSE: Entitlement and Provision*

Mike Calvert and Jenny Henderson (eds): *Managing Pastoral Care*

Steve Decker, Sandy Kirby, Angela Greenwood and Dudley Moore (eds): *Taking Children Seriously*

John McGuinness: *Counselling in Schools: New Perspectives*

Louise O'Conner, Denis O'Connor and Rachel Best (eds): *Drugs: Partnerships for Policy, Prevention and Education*

Jasper Ungoed-Thomas: *Vision of a School: The Good School in the Good Society*

CONTINUUM STUDIES IN PASTORAL CARE AND PERSONAL
AND SOCIAL EDUCATION

MEDITATION IN SCHOOLS

A PRACTICAL GUIDE TO CALMER CLASSROOMS

Edited by
Clive Erricker and Jane Erricker

Main Contributor:
Gina Levete

CONTINUUM
London and New York

Continuum

The Tower Building
11 York Road
London SE1 7NX

370 Lexington Avenue
New York
New York 10017-6503

First published 2001

British Library Cataloguing-in-Publication Data
A catalogue record for this book is available from the British Library.

ISBN: 0-8264-4977-8 (hardback)
        0-8264-4976-X (paperback)

Typeset by BookEns Ltd, Royston, Herts
Printed and bound in Great Britain by TJ International, Padstow, Cornwall

Contents

Contributors

Michael Beesley is a member of the Senior Management Team at Poole High School, Dorset. He also provides INSET courses on 'Affective Approaches to Spiritual Education'. Recently he has contributed to courses for a number of Local Education Authorities in England and in Australia. His publications include *Stilling – A Pathway for Spiritual Learning in the National Curriculum*, Salisbury Diocesan Board of Education (1990) and *Celebrating With Science*, Southgate Publishers (1993).

Jacqui Dye was special educational needs support teacher at Filton Avenue Junior School, Bristol. She is now a music adviser for the employment service in Bristol. She is also working with groups of young people outside schools on meditation.

Clive Erricker is Reader in the Study of Religions at University College Chichester. With Jane Erricker he is co-editor of the *International Journal of Children's Spirituality* and co-director of the Children and Worldviews Project (www.cwvp.ucc.ac.uk). He also publishes on religious and spiritual education.

Jane Erricker is Principal Lecturer and Science Co-ordinator in the School of Education, King Alfred's College, Winchester. With Clive Erricker she is co-editor of the *International Journal of Children's Spirituality* and co-director of the Children and Worldviews Project (www.cwvp.ucc.ac.uk). She also publishes on emotional literacy, citizenship and spiritual and moral education.

Diana Grace has pioneered meditative practice in mainstream schools since 1978. She has also run workshops in Europe, Canada and Africa. She is currently writing a book on meditation and values in education.

Gina Levete is author of *No Handicap to Dance, The Creative Tree*, and *Letting Go of Loneliness*. In 1966 she produced a report entitled *The Potential of Introducing Meditation into Schools*.

Caroline Mann works as an educational consultant specialising in counselling and learning difficulties. Her PhD dissertation was on *Meditation: Its role in education. Are children in the optimum state for effective learning?*

Nicky Newton was Religious Education Adviser to the Diocese of Salisbury. She has had extensive experience of teaching religious education in Cirencester and Gosport, Hampshire.

Leo Nolan is a Lancashire-based freelance composer, performer and teacher. He has worked with many leading community music organizations including the Hallé Orchestra's education unit. He is a trustee of the north-west-based charity Christian Meditation and a member of the World Community for Christian Meditation.

Sheela Valavi works as the London co-ordinator for the Christian Meditation Centre. Besides teaching meditation and running the London Centre she also practises head massage.

Preface

Clive Erricker, Jane Erricker, Gina Levete

Meditation in Schools is written as a resource and practical guide for class teachers and educators. Parents will find it equally valuable even though its focus is on using meditation in schools. The purpose of the book is to inspire and provide concise practical and general information and techniques that can be considered and explored before introducing primary or secondary students to meditative practice.

The book also presents an overall picture as to where meditation is practised in schools, and the perceived results. It looks at its potential to complement and aid the learning process as well as help students in their daily life. It explains the different methods of meditation and the traditions they stem from. It discusses issues and concerns involved when introducing meditation in schools. It identifies the relationship between meditation, other relaxation quietening techniques, and experiential learning. It illustrates how meditation can be applied to daily life in or out of school, and function within an holistic approach to education and growth.

The contributors to this book write from their own personal and professional practice in order to indicate what has been done as well as what can be done. In each case the aim is to show how meditation can contribute to specific school and curriculum activities, and enhance learning and educational provision generally with students of different ages and abilities. Emphasis is also placed on the enhancement of students' well-being.

Meditation is a way to help develop the positive potential of the mind and heart. In educational terms it enables both cognitive and affective development. It can radically enhance students' enjoyment of their learning and their ownership of it. For the teacher, it can significantly change the school and classroom environment in which he or she works.

The book is divided into four parts. The first part introduces meditation, explains its benefits, and identifies different types of practice. The second part goes into greater depth with respect to where and how meditation is currently practised in education, in schools and teacher education, and the relationship between meditation and important aspects of educational provision. The third and largest part identifies ways of using meditation, and other related practices, in the school, the classroom and the curriculum. The fourth part gives further reading and useful addresses.

We are grateful to our contributors for their commitment to this publication, and to Ron Best and Peter Lang for including it in their series. We hope you find it a stimulating and valuable resource. We also hope it will have some effect in changing our educational climate to one that is more respectful of the potential of the child and the teacher, and one in which schools are places 'aimed to awaken possibility'[1] rather than what Edmond Holmes described as museums:

> This school is a museum – cheerful, positive, but a museum. It describes the world as adults think it should be. The children have nothing to do here but concur and imitate.[2]

NOTES

1 This was a phrase used by Søren Kierkegaard, the nineteenth-century Danish philosopher. See Manheimer, R. J. (1977) *Kierkegaard as Educator*. Berkeley: University of California Press, p. 171.
2 Shute, C. (1998) *Edmond Holmes and 'The Tragedy of Education'*. Nottingham: Educational Heretics Press, p. 31. Edmond Holmes was the first Chief Inspector for Schools in England and Wales. Shute compares Holmes' experience to his similar experiences in schools in the 1990s.

To our children,
who are also our friends,
for their sense of humour
and ironic spirits.

Part 1:

Why Meditation?

Introduction

Gina Levete

My enthusiasm for meditation is due to a long experience of its benefits. I wish that I had been introduced to this simple practice while my family were children and teenagers. Even if they had not wished to participate they would, so to speak, have grown up within its field of influence.

A number of years ago I read an article in a national newspaper about a study that took place within a boys' school in the Middle East. A class of 15–16–year-old students were divided into groups A and B. Group A was introduced to meditation on a regular basis. In this instance, I imagine from reading the report that the purpose was to help students to concentrate and develop clarity of mind. The monitored results reported that Group A's performance, measured by the end of year exam results, had improved significantly, whereas Group B's remained as expected. I think reading this article unconsciously planted the seed of an idea.

This idea came to the surface in 1993 when I was investigating a common but sadly neglected problem – that of loneliness. It became apparent that many people from all backgrounds and walks of life, and more particularly young people, were not being helped or encouraged to enjoy occasional stillness and the solitude of their own company. In this respect, from personal experience, it seemed to me that introducing young people to meditation would help. Regardless of whether or not it had the potential to aid the process of learning, I wondered whether it had a beneficial overall role to play within the field of education, and so began a year of enquiry.

The enquiry generated an unexpected interest from both educators and parents. The findings indicated a need to share information about the practical aspects of meditation, and where and how it is practised in some schools. The enquiry also led me to make contact with Clive Erricker, whose work in religious education has included introducing students and teachers to meditation. Both of us were committed to the idea of this practice being seriously explored and considered by educators. We discussed the best way to provide the information that would enable this to happen. The eventual result, via the setting up of a meditation in education network, and making a pack available for teachers in schools, is this book.

The potential of meditation to be of benefit to young people during their primary or secondary education is generally unexplored, as is the possibility that this approach as a discipline, in the best sense of the word, could complement the process of learning. The suggestion that basic meditation could seriously be introduced as a regular part of a school programme is a relatively new idea. Understandably there can be reservations from some members of the teaching profession because little may be known about this subject and its potential application within education. It may be viewed only as something associated with new age thinking or religious belief which if imposed upon students could be harmful.

In some instances there is even a hesitancy to use the actual word 'meditation' for fear it may offend. Interestingly, older school students seem to have no problem with the word. Meditation for some is a 'right on' thing to do. For us the use of the term is important for the same reason as Deborah Rozen gives in her book *Meditating with Children: The Art of Concentration and Centering*:

> we deliberately chose to use the term 'meditating' in our title in spite of the knowledge that some educators and parents would react negatively to the word and associate it with religion ... it is important to restore meditation to its rightful definition since it is based on a rich tradition.[1]

Another understandable reservation is that there is little or no time for meditation in a busy school programme, but we have not yet found this to be a problem. For primary school children five to ten minutes once or twice a day, and for older students ten minutes once a day or fifteen to twenty minutes once a week is felt to complement rather than hinder the timetable.

Information about where meditation is practised in state and independent schools both here and in other countries is sparse and fragmented. However, where it has been introduced the feedback is encouraging. Based on students' responses and staff observation, the outcome is deemed to be positive: for example, a greater degree of calm and attentiveness was reported. At present there is practically no written evidence to support such feedback. Where meditation has been built into a school programme on an ongoing basis, it continues because it works. Perhaps this is how it should be, but for it to be seriously considered and explored by schools there is a need for written information which can be shared, and we hope this book makes a useful contribution.

NOTE

1 Rozen, D. (1994) *Meditating with Children: The Art of Concentration and Centering*. Boulder Creek, Calif.: Planetary Publications.

CHAPTER 1

Addressing inner needs

Gina Levete

Meditation has been practised for thousands of years by many cultures both in the East and West as something essential to the human spirit, but which is not necessarily dependent on 'race', history, geography or religion. It is a simple practice that focuses on the development of attention, a deep listening, attuning the body and the mind.

The primary purpose of basic meditation is to calm and stabilize both the mind and physical body, and to inspire. As such it is a practice for reflection, awareness, stillness and well-being. Meditation is sometimes equated to a royal road for personal development. This is because it is a way of working with the mind in order to be able to harness the mind's extraordinary energy and awaken it to its own natural clarity.

Before looking at how the potential of meditation, in its most practical aspect, can be of use to young people both as a tool for support and as an aid to complement the process of learning, it is important to consider how it may help to address their more *abstract* needs, such as the need to know how to stay afloat and learn to be less dependent on external and material circumstances.

In many ways it could be said that young people living in the West have never had so many opportunities to expand and explore. Generally, there is less material hardship these days. The development of technology enables them to learn more about what is going on and where. Information networks link them all over the world, and video games and virtual reality take them into worlds of fantasy.

In theory, the developing world of technology is exciting due to the impact and opportunities it can provide for society. We have more time to use our lives creatively and imaginatively, and to be concerned with the well-being of other people, plus more time for personal development and exploration. At present there is a depressing gap between theory and practice. Local communities have become increasingly separated and many people's lives are now far more isolated. Whilst enjoying the fruits of technology there is also a need to help young people understand and explore their own inner being and their relationship with the rest of nature. The present-day separation from so many natural processes can be an unconscious cause of profound loneliness, particularly for young people. Such a state of affairs may provide reasons for the remarks of these 14–16-year-old students at a comprehensive school:

'I do lots of things but inside I feel alone.'
'I hate doing nothing.'
'I go to lots of parties but sometimes I wonder what it's about.'
'I always have the radio on for background noise.'
'Walking is boring unless there is something at the end of it.'

As adults we now have more opportunities than ever before to balance the surfeit of external distraction and attraction. For ourselves we may recognize the need to nourish the spirit in other ways through meditation, classes, groups, books, exercise, teachers. Adults can explore the mystical, the religious, the spiritual, the peaceful, the alternative across the world without having to leave the country. Through the wonder of technology we are exposed to the great religious traditions of the world, and the great philosophies or approaches to life from Native American Indian culture to that of the Inuit. Even so, perhaps nine times out of ten these opportunities to balance the external and inner world only occur by chance; often we stumble upon them late in life. How much easier adult life might be if these openings were part of a rounded education.

Deborah Rozen in her excellent book *Meditating with Children* writes:

> While many programmes are available to adults who seek to integrate their mental, physical and spiritual natures through groups, teachers, books etc. ... it didn't make sense to me that children spend the first twenty years of their lives learning ineffective ways to deal with life, and spend the next twenty years trying to unlearn them if they ever do.[1]

Nowadays, a greater number of schools, particularly at primary level, introduce considered approaches which encourage students to handle and express their emotions. Circle time is an example where students are helped to learn the art of listening to what someone else has to say and respecting that viewpoint, as well as having the confidence to present their own clearly. Stilling, guided imagery, and yoga are recognized methods used for quietening and relaxation. Mathew Lipman's work at Columbia University, and his two books *Philosophy Goes to School*[2] and *Thinking in Education*[3] have influenced some teachers to place a greater emphasis on encouraging students to develop their capacity to reason, reflect and debate.

The question may arise, after this, whether there is really any need for meditation. The suggestion is yes, because, as a practice, it will complement and enhance these other initiatives and provide a missing piece in the jigsaw. Meditation works directly with the mind, either drawing attention beyond usual mental activity to deeper levels of rest and clarity, or to gently teach the mind to develop the habit of attentive awareness in daily life.

Most of us, whether young or old, need help to know how to do this; how to absorb and be more acutely aware of those qualities which create a sense of wholeness and well-being. These are abstract qualities which have no material existence. They are similar, in this respect, to a quality like beauty. In some way all of us have a longing to connect with beauty; yet it only arises from the beholder's consciousness of it. Therefore a young person's need may not only be to have opportunities to be exposed to beautiful objects or surroundings, but the means to know how to absorb them; in other words how to receive or have a beautiful experience. Peace is also an abstract quality, yet peace of mind is the jewel in the crown of life. In this instance students may need a method which helps them to tap into stillness and peace.

The late Chogyam Trungpa, a Tibetan meditation master who, through his writings, clearly seemed to sense the needs of the Western mind, describes how through the practice of meditation we can at any age develop a greater sensitivity, a basic compassion, what he calls 'the awakened heart'.[4] Words that describe abstract states such as awakened heart, awe, wonder, inspiration are natural states to the very young, but generally for anyone over the age of seven they are out of fashion. From an early age we are encouraged to think only from the head rather than also with the heart. Ninety-nine per cent of the time the emphasis is on doing, rather than being.

Meditation is about being. As one teacher put it 'being no one, going nowhere.'[5] To learn how to simply be, and rest with the moment, sounds easy in theory, but in practice it may be difficult because of the constant emphasis on activity which creates a restlessness within us all. Meditation practice can offer students an approach to help address the abstract needs of their inner being. Its discipline, in the best sense of the word, involves stillness and silence. From this position there can be a space for peace, wonder and awe.

NOTES

1 Rozen, D. (1994) *Meditation with Children: The Art of Concentration and Centering*. Boulder Creek, Calif.: Planetary Publications, pp. 1–2.
2 Lipman, M. (1988) *Philosophy Goes to School*. Philadelphia: Temple University Press.
3 Lipman, M. (1991) *Thinking in Education*. Cambridge: Cambridge University Press.
4 Trungpa, Chogyam (1973) *Cutting Through Spiritual Materialism*. Berkeley, Calif.: Shambala.
5 Khema, Ayya (1987) *Being Nobody, Going Nowhere*. London: Wisdom Publications.

CHAPTER 2

A support for everyday life
Gina Levete

This chapter looks at meditation as a practical self-help approach. An approach that could perhaps equip each young person for the rest of their lives with a simple practice not only to nourish their spirit, but also to alleviate physical and mental stress: self-help to discover a core of inner strength and the freedom of self-reliance.

Any method of meditation is simply a framework that may make it easier to rest in a period of silence and quiet. It can provide a formal structure to help instil a greater sense of calm, well-being, awakened awareness and clarity of mind.

Our present-day trends suggest that in order to find support and solutions it is necessary to look outside ourselves. Helplines and counselling are a growing industry. Few people, if any, can be an island unto themselves, but in each of us there is an often unexplored core of inner strength waiting to emerge. At this present time is there enough encouragement given to young people to discover that core, and the freedom and dignity of self-reliance?

Just as the oak tree may have to stand alone in the field at some point in its life, so might any young person. Do they understand that some people can be relied upon, but not others, and that ultimately their own best friend and teacher has to be themselves? Is there sufficient guidance on the art of self-help; guidance such that the child, the adolescent and the adult can journey through life intact while traversing the polarities of positive and negative effects, influences and emotions? We all need such guidance and support in order to be able to pick ourselves up, dust ourselves down, and keep on going.

From an early age most of us have been conditioned to regard our negative emotions as unnatural states of mind to be covered over either through suppression or distraction. Contrastingly, positive feelings such as peace, happiness and goodwill should always be a natural, permanent state of being. In reality, the positive image of what we should or should not be thinking, doing or feeling does not work out that way; thought is often in a crisis of conflict: confused, guilty and deeply afraid. A negative experience is often regarded as unnatural, a personal affront, or personal failure.

Though this conditioned viewpoint is understandable, since nobody wishes to suffer, it can be the cause of yet more conflict and pain to a young or older mind. A consequence of this way of thinking is that habitual thought patterns are divorced from a deeper level of intuitive understanding; an understanding which recognizes and accepts its interdependent connection with the rest of nature. By realizing that, as an interdependent expression of this wonderful incomprehensible thing called life, we too, the physical body and the process of thought, are subject to its natural laws, most particularly the laws of polarity, positive and negative, impermanence and change, we come to understand our experiences differently.

Habitually, in order to avoid the truth of the moment, especially if it is something difficult to acknowledge, the mind develops the habit of 'leap-frogging' the present. Much adult emphasis, relayed to children, focuses on striving towards images and concepts of what should or should not be. Our thoughts become engaged in writing a script that may never happen, without attending to how we cope in the moments when it fails. Facing the truth of the moment, however uncomfortable, necessarily results in acknowledging the fact of what is, rather than an idea of what ought to be, or how we wish things to be. In an awareness of the present, of how things are, it can be much easier to be one's own person and manage the present situation effectively.

We may ask the question, 'What has this adult perspective to do with young people?' The suggestion is that if young people can be helped to understand and accept their interdependent connection with the rest of animate and inanimate life, and the natural laws that govern this connection, they can develop greater resilience to face and work with the way things are. The introduction of meditation can be an effective way to learn how to do this, for it is a practice which helps the mind to develop the habit of being in the present moment, to be aware of the now, the what is.

PRACTICAL BENEFITS

The uncomfortable situations young people face are numerous. Rejection by a best friend may bring hurt temporarily pushed away, but not dealt with. Silent anger or jealousy directed at a brother or sister may bring guilt which is covered up, but somehow sticks around as a whisper. Wishing to look like someone else rather than the way you do causes low self-esteem to creep in. Not knowing how to say no to group pressure when invited to smoke, take drugs, have sex, or make racist jokes can result in unwilling and uncomfortable compromise. Being too shy to be sociable may develop into a sense of being the constant outsider. The list goes on and on, not only for young people but adults too, particularly if we still feel ten years old inside.

The purpose of meditation practice is to benefit not only the period of quiet sitting, but also to benefit the rest of the day and such experiences as those illustrated above. Verbal feedback from students who have been introduced to different methods of meditation at school indicates that this can be so. As part of an enquiry into meditation in schools, students of different ages and different backgrounds were invited to express their views about meditation.[1] Some students attended state schools, others independent ones. Their overall perspectives were remarkably similar. Most of them preferred to regard meditation as a spiritual practice, 'though not religious', which also was of therapeutic and practical benefit.

The two practical benefits they were most enthusiastic about were that they had found it could be a way to help them acknowledge and handle their emotions, particularly the unwanted ones, and its potential as an approach to relieve stress. They responded with comments such as: 'peaceful', 'calming', 'not stressed out', 'helps you go to sleep at night'.

Madeleine Simon, a Catholic nun who introduces children to a practice of Christian meditation, says in her book *Born Contemplative*, 'Meditation is slowly being understood and not feared as religion but a simple technique at its most superficial level to help reduce stress and tap into stillness.'[2]

A small group of students at a sixth-form college in a deprived multiracial area of London was introduced to meditation by their dance teacher, who is someone who has practised meditation for a number of years. None of these students had any previous exposure to meditation. Once or twice a week at the start of each class they were invited to meditate for fifteen minutes. After calming the body and mind by sitting and focusing their attention on the rhythmic pattern of their breathing, they sat, or rather in this instance lay down, and impartially observed the mind's stream of thoughts without intervention or judgement. When asked how they felt about doing this, the general response was gratitude for having been introduced to a way of acknowledging themselves 'which didn't make me feel guilty about what I sometimes think'. One girl said now she tried to apply the same approach when things were difficult between her and her mother and father, 'so I don't flare up'.

Out of four hundred pupils at a well-known coeducational boarding school in Hampshire, just twelve 13–16-year-old students chose meditation as their voluntary activity. These weekly sessions lasted for an hour and were led by the music teacher, who had practised meditation for a number of years. Each session began with walking meditation, followed by quiet sitting with the focus on the breath. The last part of the session was a general discussion. With two exceptions, the students' overall view was that these periods of voluntary activity gave them food for thought, with comments such as 'Helps you to look at things in different ways'. They found the practice of walking meditation particularly helpful because it was 'freeing'. Some said they often did it when getting from one classroom to another because it 'helps you not to feel so rushed'.

The preparatory school to this senior school explored the introduction of meditation through a different route. After obtaining their parents' permission, twelve 11–13-year-old boys and girls, who had again chosen meditation as their voluntary activity, visited a nearby Buddhist monastery. Once a week for one term the students and their two teachers were introduced by a Buddhist monk to walking and standing meditation, reconnecting with the body, as well as sitting meditation when the breath was the object of attention. Four of the twelve students dropped out. One girl said 'I didn't find meditation did anything for me.' The other three felt uncomfortable sitting silently 'for such a long time'. The remaining eight students who stayed the ten weeks spoke with enthusiasm about the practical application of the practice. 'Like when breaking with a friend', 'angry', 'stressed out', 'yes if I'm worried', 'I don't like cricket, and if I do standing meditation I get over minding not liking cricket'. They were also enthusiastic about the way the monk introduced it 'so that anyone could do it, you didn't have to be Buddhist'.

The comments of other students indicated the value of a general discussion after the period of quiet sitting that allows young people the opportunity to question and explore. 'The depth of thought relating to those questions we all ask and long to know amazed me', is how one English teacher described the outcome of the discussion period with 16-year-old girls. Sadly, when this teacher left, the sessions came to an end. Another teacher, using visualization as the method, followed through periods of quiet sitting by inviting her students at this state primary school to continue meditation through the expression of silent drawing or painting.

The views of the students who spoke about their personal experiences of meditation demonstrate that a method can provide a formal structure to help the young mind to help itself. Like the boy who practised standing meditation to help him 'not mind not liking cricket'. He was not saying 'to help me like cricket', but to face the fact that he did not, and find a way to come to terms with this. The sixth-form student who utilized the impartial approach of observing the thought process when she and her parents fell out found a new way to acknowledge and handle her emotions with less conflict and guilt. The majority of students said they benefited from the therapeutic aspect of the practice as a means to alleviate stress. There were students who found, as one girl said, that 'meditation did nothing for me' but in each school they were in the minority.

The quietness and bearing of the adult who introduces meditation to young people is crucial, as is the teacher's own belief in the value of the practice and their skill in communicating this to students. The examples mentioned demonstrate that it is these qualities which enabled students to recognize that a method of meditation is beneficial and relevant not only during the period of quiet but throughout the day. In other words each of these students on their own terms and in their own way has been able to extract from the structure of a method its essence, and apply this to their particular needs. They are beginning to discover their inner core of strength, and the freedom of self-reliance.

NOTES

1   This enquiry resulted in the research report (1987) 'Presenting the case for meditation in primary and secondary schools'. The first part of this book is based on the findings of that research with the addition of further material from the study in chapter 6.
2   Simon, M. (1993) *Born Contemplative*. London: Darton, Longman & Todd (now only available from Medio Media).

CHAPTER 3

Meditation for health and well-being

Gina Levete

INTRODUCTION

This chapter looks at the practical aspect of meditation as a means to improve or sustain good health. The introduction of meditation as part of a regimen for health care is now being acknowledged in a number of instances as an aid to complement standard medical treatments. Controlled studies with adult patients provide evidence of the efficacy of this practice in relieving stress, hypertension, high blood pressure, the compulsive tendencies of an addiction, depression and epilepsy. It is also now being considered a practice that can help young people with behavioural difficulties. One national health therapist who introduced meditation to a group of hyperactive children between the ages of eight and eleven spoke of the potential of meditation as 'profoundly important'. This sentiment is supported by a teacher working in a secondary school with as she put it 'disaffected students'.

In the West there is a tendency to live life intellectually, up in the head rather than as a total body. Young or old, for any of us it makes complete sense to learn how to harmonize and quieten the physical body and mental activity. The structure of a simple method of meditation can enable this to happen. What is more, unlike pill popping, there are no likely side effects other than a greater sense of personal control, calm and well-being.

THE THERAPEUTIC EFFECTS OF MEDITATION

Why has meditation not been more widely advocated in relation to health and well-being? Within the field of medicine until recently little has been known about the subject and its therapeutic application. There have been, and perhaps still are, some professional reservations, or even resistance to this approach, because it is perceived as something only to do with religion or new age thinking which, if imposed upon a patient, could be an intrusion. Another reason is that in the areas of health care where it has been introduced, there has been little opportunity to share the positive feedback through lack of a network for the dissemination of such information. Happily, along with other complementary therapies the picture is beginning to change.

In relation to the health and well-being of students, William Linden of the Bureau of Child Guidance, Brooklyn, New York, submitted a paper entitled 'Practising of meditation by school children and their levels of field independence, test anxiety, and reading achievement' (1973). This study was based on a dissertation as part of the requirements of a Ph.D. and submitted to the School of Education in New York. The author explains:

> The study was performed in a school in an economically disadvantaged neighbourhood of blacks and Puerto Ricans. The school administration placed children in third-grade classes mainly on the basis of their reading scores at the end of second grade ... Nine boys and nine girls were picked at random. Of these three boys and three girls from each class were randomly assigned to one of the three treatment conditions: meditation group, guidance group, and a group remaining with the rest of the class receiving no special attention outside the classroom. The meditation group practised two exercises: one for 10–15 minutes, the other for five to ten minutes ... the meditation group gained on the measure of field independence and reduced on the measure of test anxiety ... The central aim of this study was to determine whether children could be trained in the practice of meditation and to examine the effects such training might have on selected aspects of their cognitive and effective functioning. The results confirm children can be taught this discipline and apparently with beneficial results ... The results encourage further investigation of meditation as a training method of self-discovery and self-mastery.[1]

In 1989 Vivekananda Kendra Yoga Research Foundation, Bangalore, India, undertook a study entitled 'The integrated approach of yoga, a therapeutic tool for mentally retarded children; a one-year controlled study'. Ninety children with mild, moderate and severe learning difficulties were selected from four special schools in Bangalore. Forty-five children underwent five hours a week yogic training which included breathing exercises, loosening exercises and meditation. Comparisons were made before and after training with the 45 students who were not exposed to this training but continued their usual school routine. The authors reported:

> There was a highly significant improvement in the IQ and social adaptation parameters in the yogic group as compared to the control group. This study shows the efficacy of yoga as an effective therapeutic tool in the management of mentally retarded children.[2]

The Appalachian State University in North Carolina produced a study entitled 'Meditation and college students, self-actualization and rated stress'. This study involved 62 college students. Two groups were given mantra meditation and a yogic relaxation technique referred to as Shavasana. The report stated:

> There were significant scores on self-actualization: however no differences were found between the groups. Meditation training was associated with larger gains in scores on measures of systematic relaxed behaviour, than of the relaxation training.[3]

Other studies, such as those in relation to health, which are available in précis form via the Internet, describe the positive results of introducing the practice of mindfulness or Transcendental Meditation to help patients cope with various illnesses. When considering the potential of meditation for students the therapeutic aspect should also be taken into account, for a simple method can provide a means of self-help towards health and well-being.

NOTES

1 Linden, William (1973) Practising of meditation by school children and their levels of field independence, test anxiety, and reading achievement, *Journal of Consulting and Clinical Psychology*, **41**(1), 139–43.
2 Uma, K., Nagendra Nagarathna, H. R., Vaidehi, S., Seethalakshmi, R. (1989) The integrated approach of yoga, a therapeutic tool for mentally retarded children; a one-year controlled study, *Journal of Mental Deficiency Research*, January.
3 Janowiak, J. and Hackman, R. (1994) Meditation and college students, self-actualization and rated stress, *Psychol Rep QF6*, October.

CHAPTER 4

Meditation to develop mindfulness in daily life

Gina Levete

THE ATTENTIVE MIND

The attentive mind is an awakened mind, possessing heightened awareness. It opens the door to the depth of the silent mind. Self-confidence grows because there is space for a more controlled collected process of thought and physical action. The word *attention* conjures different images, some of which may be associated with a somewhat rigid or forced state of being. Sometimes the word can be associated with regret. 'If only I had paid more attention', the inference being that a negative outcome might have been prevented. The Oxford Dictionary's definition describes a different intent behind the word: 'Applying oneself' – mental concentration, 'attentions' – small acts of courtesy, 'attentive' – paying attention, watchful devotion, showing consideration or courtesy to another person, 'mindful' – taking thought or care of something. Rather than as only reaction to an external directive, attention or attentiveness is a giving from within, an openness to the immediate. These modest words describe the potential of a human mind to wholeheartedly apply itself to any situation with concern, generosity and respect.

Mindfulness fosters spontaneity and immediacy, characteristics which are often lost in adult life. By nature the young are immediate and spontaneous, but these attractive qualities can lead to heedlessness and problems if there is no guidance for the need for them to be conjoined with mindfulness.

Mind: (1) the ability to be aware of things and to think and reason, originating in the brain, (2) a person's thoughts and attention, (3) remembrance. Here the Oxford Dictionary's definitions of mind describe an overall mental state that is often described as mindfulness. Concentration is generally associated with the ability to focus on a subject one-pointedly to the exclusion of all else, whereas mindfulness is being aware of all that is happening, like a bird perched high in a tree surveying the surrounds from its vantage point. This is not some unusual state of being, but rather a natural one, waiting to function freed of the crowded, easily distracted habits of the 'grasshopper' mind. It is a state in which there is less likelihood of harming or being harmed. A state where negative thought or behaviour can be restrained.

Whether young or old, the unfocused habits of the scattered mind are no one's best friend, particularly when it comes to personal well-being. The busy, crowded mind tends to cut corners in relation to just about everything. The results amongst other things can be over-reaction, hasty judgement, and heedless action. Situations are created where thought appears to control the thinker rather than the other way about. When the young mind is open and pliable it can more easily absorb new habits such as the power of attention. This attention is not just for the purpose of absorbing information, but also to develop a more protective state of being.

Meditation is an inroad to mindfulness. Usually it is only associated with a formal period of silent sitting, but that is just one structure. Cultivating the habit of mindfulness in daily life is in itself a form of meditation. In theory it sounds easy to do, in practice it can be difficult because of the complexity of an easily distracted mind. It is suggested that mindfulness could be introduced to students as a subject in its own right, rather than pegged on as an afterthought to a particular situation that may have led a young person into trouble. Mental and physical mindfulness go hand-in-hand, and can be practised when walking, sitting or carrying out a daily task (see Chapter 12). If being mindful sounds too complicated, the word watchful rather than mindful perhaps may be more easily understood.

To question whether this approach is conducive to the high energy levels of students is understandable, but perhaps it underestimates their capacity to try out new suggestions, particularly if the practical applications and likely benefits are explained to them.

THE REASONING MIND

Philosophy: the Oxford Dictionary describes this as the search for logical reasoning, for understanding of the basic truths and principles of the universe, life and morals, and of human perception and understanding of these. Helping students to reason, reflect and debate is of increasing interest to mainstream education. As mentioned previously, a prominent influence in introducing young and older students to philosophical debate is the work and books of Mathew Lipman in the United States, and in the UK there is the Society for the Advancement of Philosophical Enquiry and Reflection in Education (SAPERE). SAPERE runs courses for primary and secondary schoolteachers wishing to learn more about this.[1] The accounts of teachers, and the remarks of the students from the very young to sixth-form level, highlight the value of such debate, which in itself is a practice of mindfulness. Philosophical debate is often ignored, or seen as peripheral to discussion on more tangible political and social issues; yet without the opportunity to explore and question the philosophical and spiritual, education is incomplete, and given such opportunities students can be breathtakingly original and wise.

So far there has been no direct connection between this and the development of meditation, but the analogy is close. It is suggested that now these strands need to be introduced in tandem.

CONCLUSION

With older students, practising mindfulness may be a somewhat self-conscious exercise initially. With help and perseverance it becomes less and less so, until one day the habit seems to happen by itself, if not all the time at least some of the time. That is when mindfulness begins to take the position of individual and public protector.

NOTE

1 For information on SAPERE courses or INSET contact Roger Sutcliffe, North Mead House, 3 North Mead, Puriton, Somerset TA7 8DD.

CHAPTER 5

Different methods of meditation

Gina Levete

BASIC MEDITATION: WHAT IS INVOLVED?

Meditation is often associated with the religions of both the East and West. Without in any way imposing a particular philosophy or belief, the same simple methods can be introduced and adapted to help young people learn how to meditate from an early age. Meditation does not presume a particular faith or non-faith stance but is a means to calming the mind and acquiring insight into the nature of experience and how the mind works. However, it is not possible to demonstrate this without doing it for yourself.

The purpose of meditation is not only to be of benefit during the time of practice; the benefits can apply to the rest of the day. It is not about forcing the mind to concentrate, to be still and empty of thought, or striving to achieve a particular result. On the contrary, the whole purpose of meditation is to learn to let go, to allow things to be as they are – to experience the moment as it is, and to develop a greater sense of inner stillness and peace.

Meditation is usually practised in a sitting position, with emphasis on posture. It can also be done lying down, or through a physical activity such as walking. A simple method can be taught in a short time.

For very young children, meditation might only last for five minutes once or twice a day; and for older students ten to fifteen minutes, or fifteen to twenty minutes once a week. The quality of the sitting periods is more important than the length of time. The more regular the practice, the greater are the benefits. Initially, it is very important that someone skilled in this practice should introduce it into a school setting, either directly to the students or to the teachers.

DIFFERENT METHODS OF MEDITATION

It is not this chapter's purpose to advocate any one method of meditation. Everyone may feel that the method they adopt is the most effective. Having observed students in different schools practising different ways of meditation, the overall impression is that each method in its own way produces a positive effect:

Following the breath
Following the breath helps to calm and focus the mind quickly, and to stabilize the body. The object of attention is the breath. Meditators are shown how to focus gently on the natural rhythm of the breath, inhalation and exhalation. The point of attention is usually either the tip of the nostrils or just below the navel. After breathing in and out deeply a few times the meditator sits quietly and focuses on the breath as it enters and leaves the body in its own rhythm. In theory this sounds an easy thing to do; in practice it can be difficult to sustain the focus for more than a few breaths. Once this simple technique has been learnt however, it can be applied at any time, especially at times of stress.

Connecting to the body
The object of attention is the body. The meditator learns to come down from the 'thinking head' to sit as the 'total body'. The instructor guides the meditator on how to connect with different parts of the body, and then to be aware of the whole body and its ceaseless work carried out without any conscious instruction. The meditator, as the 'total body', sits peacefully aware of the body breathing, renewing and repairing itself from moment to moment.

Walking meditation
The object of attention is the action of slow walking. Total attention is placed in the action of the feet as they move and connect with the ground, harmonizing the action of walking step by step with the breath.

Meditation on a sound or word: mantra meditation
The object of attention is simply a sound or word. Under the initial guidance of a teacher this is silently repeated over and over again until the mind is focused and settles in quietness, beyond the usual realm of mental activity, into attentive wakefulness. Christian meditation and meditation of other faiths use a word with meaning. Transcendental Meditation (TM) introduces a sound without conceptual meaning or image.

Meditation and visualization
Under the guidance of a teacher, this method uses visualization as a way for meditators to become more aware of their own potential and positive qualities. For example, the meditator may visualize the body filled with light, the warmth of the sun, or with positive qualities such as kindness, patience or goodwill held in the mind or directed outwards to other people. This can be remarkably effective in inspiring the realization of one's own goodness. It can be particularly encouraging for deprived children to be aware of what they can offer other people.

Meditation observing the mind
Although this is perhaps the most effective way of developing a sense of equanimity, it is a more advanced technique that requires a longer period of instruction, and is thus suitable only for older students. Here the object of attention is the mind's stream of thought. The meditator sits peacefully observing the flow of thought passing through the mind without the

intervention of judgement, attachment or suppression. Instead, each passing thought is simply noted with its impermanence, when there is no conscious interference or attachment to it.

DIFFERENCES BETWEEN MEDITATION AND OTHER QUIETING TECHNIQUES

Nowadays, meditation is a commonly used word to describe a wide range of practices. Consequently, it conjures up different images for different people. It differs from approaches such as stilling methods, guided imagery, or quiet moments after the practice of yoga or circle time. Pointing to a difference is not to imply that meditation is better or more needed than these other approaches: it is simply to say that it is a different discipline.

Perhaps the main difference between meditation and other quietening techniques is one of focus. Meditation works directly with the mind: it either draws the attention beyond the usual mental activity to deeper levels of rest and clarity, or gently trains and tames the mind to develop concentration and the habit of attentive awareness in daily life.

MEDITATION AS VISUALIZATION COMPARED TO GUIDED IMAGERY

The question is often asked about the difference between guided imagery – which is frequently introduced by class teachers in primary schools – and meditation as visualization. It is important for teachers to understand the distinction. In the religious traditions, meditation as visualization is usually practised to inspire the meditator to be aware inwardly of his or her own potential for goodness and transcendence, or to develop concentration. Images or qualities such as love, generosity, wisdom or light filling the body are visualized under the guidance of a teacher. The purpose of the process is to look within in order to give out. Generally, however, guided imagery takes the imagination on an external journey, and is practised within the context of experiential learning.

Part 2:

Meditation in Education

CHAPTER 6

Meditation as it is practised in education

Gina Levete

The following synopsis and examples are an indication of the present overall picture of meditation in state and independent schools, and augment the material found in Chapter 2. Although new information continues to be collected, it seems to support rather than alter the picture. The following few examples of current meditation practice in schools reflect the different meditation methods described in Chapter 5. When reading about the way meditation is practised in independent schools based on the values of a particular religion or philosophy, readers are respectfully asked to keep an open mind. Otherwise, without further exploration, there may be an assumption that the particular method is only appropriate within the context of that school.

Information about where meditation is practised in state and independent schools both in the UK and other countries is sparse and fragmented. Its potential to complement and aid the process of learning has hardly been looked at. Where it has been introduced, the feedback is encouraging. Based on the students' responses and staff observation the outcome is recognized as beneficial: for example, a greater degree of calm and attentiveness was reported. At present, with the exception of Caroline Mann's study (see Chapters 7 and 8), there is practically no carefully researched written evidence to support this verbal feedback. Where meditation is built into the school programme on an ongoing basis it just continues to happen because it works. Perhaps this is as it should be, but there is a need for this evidence to be shared if the subject is to be seriously considered within the broader field of education.

Different approaches such as yoga, stilling, guided imagery, meditation and circle time are introduced in state schools, particularly at primary level, to help students relax, quieten, learn to listen, express and handle their emotions.

It needs to be emphasized again that in presenting the case for meditation the suggestion is not that it should replace other excellent and needed approaches. Instead, meditation can have a distinct and useful role to play alongside these practices. This is particularly important at secondary level.

Where meditation has been introduced but not built in as a regular part of a school programme, it appears to be a positive but brief experience that happens almost by chance. This has often been because it was suggested to the school by someone skilled in introducing children to meditation and prepared to do it on a voluntary basis for a short time. However positive the results have been when the meditation instructor leaves, there has been little or no discussion about how it can be followed through. One teacher respected for the way she introduces children to meditation worked for three years in a state primary school on a voluntary basis. The weekly sessions where students between the ages of seven and nine meditated and then were invited to continue the meditation through the expression of painting, were acknowledged by the school to be of real benefit. Despite this, at the end of the three years the sessions ceased. It may be that introducing meditation on a somewhat *ad hoc* basis results in it being regarded as something nice but divorced from the process of education.

Where meditation is built in as a regular part of a school programme there is far greater opportunity for it to be of lasting benefit. In this respect, perhaps independent schools including those teaching mainstream traditional methods are a little more adventurous., Haberdashers Aske, a well-known mainstream independent school for boys, introduced meditation as a result of the visit of a Franciscan friar in 1986. Since then the school has offered a fifteen minute once a week lunchtime meditation session open to any boy who wishes to participate. The numbers range from six to thirty-six students. There are also meditation sessions for entire classes as part of the students' experience of learning about Buddhism. 'Meditation is, I am sure, of enormous educational as well as spiritual value' (School Chaplain, Haberdashers Aske School).

Instances of meditation being practised in state secondary schools are rare. If it occurs at all it is generally as a brief experience included as part of a course on world religions. Where secondary or sixth-form students have the opportunity to meditate the result appears to be wholly positive. So much more seems to be offered to primary school children than older students. However there is perhaps an even greater need for secondary students to be helped to manage and express emotion, to recognize their inner strength, and their ability to help themselves.

Given the right climate, opportunity and support, no one group of students is more or less able to meditate than another. Students are students the world over. Regardless of background, culture or religion, young people instinctively seem able to understand the practice although initially not all may find it an easy thing to do. There is a place for meditation in state schools just as there is in independent mainstream schools, or those schools whose teaching is based on the spiritual values of a particular religion, teacher or philosophy.

STATE SCHOOLS

In the few primary schools where meditation has been introduced it usually takes the form of focusing on the breath or visualization (see Chapter 5) followed by discussion, painting or a story. The actual period of silence lasts about five to ten minutes. The children are encouraged to be aware of their own positive qualities, to wonder, and explore.

A ten-week pilot project was carried out at a London primary school in the East End. For one term a class of eight- and nine-year-old children were introduced to between five and ten minutes meditation through visualization. Diana Grace, the visiting teacher who led the sessions, was someone experienced in introducing meditation to very young children and their teachers. Some of the children were quite disruptive and found the idea of stillness disconcerting and difficult, though less so by the end of ten weeks. After the last session the class teacher, who had herself participated, invited the students to write or draw their thoughts on meditation. Michael and Tina wrote:

> Meditation with Diana is peaceful like when you get out of bed, turn off the TV and get a tape that is a relaxing tape. When I meditate I think about the summer holidays before we were in class.
> Michael.

> When I close my eyes I don't see anything, but when I open and close them I do see something, and on Thursday I saw a river in my meditation and I saw four colours in the river – red, green, orange and yellow.
> Tina.

Diana explained the type of meditation she used and its intention:

> The meditation I was facilitating at St Paul's School was one whereby children were being encouraged into becoming more aware of their inner essence. It is my usual practice with children after meditation that they have an opportunity to send out love to people of their choice, to areas of conflict in the world and to give thanks to creation, people of their choosing and the life within them.

When Diana left the sessions ceased, although the class teacher hoped to incorporate some of the ideas.

Clive Erricker's courses for teachers demonstrate that it is possible to introduce a practice from a religious tradition that will be useful to the students in the larger context without the ideology. His work with primary children includes story, ritual and meditation. A similar programme was introduced for children who were emotionally disturbed.

Meditation is now being seriously looked at as a way of helping young and older people who have behavioural or emotional difficulties. The Home Office supports the work of The Prison Phoenix Trust in introducing yoga and meditation to inmates, and occasionally young offenders. The director of this organization has the interesting background of being both a Catholic nun and a Zen Buddhist teacher.

An NHS therapist who has herself meditated for many years, introduced meditation to 8–10-year-old emotionally disturbed children in an assessment centre in the North of England. She wrote:

> I consider it a valuable experience for them to be part of a quiet centred and internally centred co-operative group. I found that 'old hands' freely helped new children to settle ... Feedback after meditation was very positive, feelings of calm happiness etc., being described ... Although the

boundary between relaxation and meditation was very fine, I always kept a 'meditation' attitude myself.

In state primary schools, and particularly church schools, stilling or silence is often introduced as part of collective worship. The fine line between this and meditation has already been addressed. A number of projects such as the Manchester-based 'Values and Visions', and the 'Hope Project' in the West Midlands, whose origins stem from the Quaker movement, have worked with teachers introducing them to methods which encourage stillness.

It is not all plain sailing when introducing meditation in state schools. As previously mentioned, the word 'meditation' is often misunderstood or feared. A dance teacher who also teaches meditation spoke about her work at a London sixth-form college. With the approval of the head of department, students between the ages of 16 and 20 have a weekly twenty-minute period of meditation as part of their course in movement. She advocates this practice because of the noticeable and positive feedback from the students. Yet despite this, other members of the staff dismiss the whole idea as 'new age stuff'. The teacher expressed her concern at having little contact with others working in education who are interested in a spiritual as well as academic emphasis. A teacher introducing yoga and meditation to primary students at a Dublin school with the full approval of the school's principal, received anonymous letters accusing her of 'creating a space to let the devil in'. The principal of a secondary school invited a university lecturer to give a one-off talk on Buddhism on the understanding that the subject of meditation was not brought up, let alone practised.

Such rigid and subjective viewpoints are the exception rather than the rule. A more common reaction is the anxiety that meditation may be imposing a particular religious belief or philosophy on students. The potential of formal meditation to aid and complement the learning process is a relatively new suggestion. At present there is little or no general information about the subject relative to the area of education which could help to allay these concerns.

INDEPENDENT SCHOOLS

The overall general picture is similar to that of state schools, though perhaps if a decision is taken to introduce meditation on an ongoing basis there is more flexibility, making it easier to put into practice. A number of independent schools such as the John Scottus School (Ireland), St James Independent School for Boys and Girls (London), and the Pluto School (the Netherlands), introduce students from the age of ten onwards to regular meditation based on the method known as Transcendental Meditation. These schools advocate the benefits of meditation and this method in particular. All three schools are based on the spiritual values and philosophy of the founders of the schools. At St James and at John Scottus the academic teaching is traditional mainstream. The following comments illustrate the views of members of staff:

'Some of the students put their lack of fear at exam time down to meditation.'

'It is a part of the spiritual education among other kinds of concentration, exercises and philosophy.'

'At ten they take to it like ducks to water, at sixteen they analyse and question the practice.'

At St James all the staff practise the same method of meditation. This school has students from varying faiths such as Jewish, Moslem, Christian and Hindu, and parents are asked for their permission before students are introduced to this method of meditation. The younger students aged four to ten at St James School are prepared for meditation by the attractive idea of introducing a few moments of stillness and silence after each activity throughout the day. This simple idea can have a positive effect in developing a sense of calm. If it does not already happen in primary school this could be a simple and easy practice to introduce. Meditation sessions at John Scottus are voluntary, but the principal says ninety per cent of the boys choose to attend.

Mantra meditation is practised at the Sunrise Primary School. This less orthodox small school is based in one of the most deprived London areas, with a richly mixed ethnic population reflected by its students. Again the school is based around the philosophy/religion of a particular teacher. Forty per cent of the parents who send their children follow the same philosophy/religion. The local education authority occasionally refers disruptive children attending a mainstream state primary to the school. The principal said that at first such children found it very difficult to settle, 'but come again in six weeks and you will notice a difference'.

Here the children are introduced to stillness at the age of three years old. By the age of six each day begins with a fifteen minute period of meditation. The method offered is the silent repetition of a word that has an inspiring meaning. This is similar to a form of meditation sometimes practised within the Christian tradition and described by Madeleine Simon in *Born Contemplative*,[1] but somewhat different from the method known as Transcendental Meditation.

The practice starts by singing a word that is associated with well-being. The children sing the word to guitar music for two or three minutes. Then sitting in meditation posture they silently focus their attention for ten minutes. It was noticeable how after five minutes of quiet sitting these six- to eleven-year-old pupils seemed to reach a state of peace and stillness which was neither forced nor rigid. After the session it was possible to talk to the children on their own. Asked how they felt about meditation their enthusiasm was directed to the fact it helped them to feel 'peaceful' and was a useful practice to turn to if things were difficult, 'like when you get angry', as one boy said. Asked if meditation practice was ever helpful outside school when things went wrong, the response was lively. Almost all said 'yes' and supported this with a personal story. Many of these children were exposed to meditation at home because the parents followed the same spiritual philosophy.

In conclusion, the benefits of different types of meditation can be seen in the examples described where this practice can and does help young people, not only during the time of practice, but within the context of their daily life. There are indications also that meditation can improve academic performance. For there to be more effective and systematic use of this practice it needs the interest and involvement of teachers and others established within the field of education, and social and pastoral care. Without this the picture will remain fragmented, and will continue only to benefit a few students who have the opportunity to be introduced to meditation and assess the results for themselves.

NOTE

1   Simon, Madeleine (1993) *Born Contemplative*. London: Darton, Longman & Todd.

CHAPTER 7

The potential of meditation in education

Caroline Mann

The interest in meditation as a technique for training the mind is gathering momentum. A review of the literature on meditation reveals that although there is a wealth of information written on the various types and methods of meditation available for adults, there is comparatively little written on meditation with children in education.[1] In order to look at the potential of meditation in education it is essential to first attempt to define what is meant by the term.

WHAT ACTUALLY IS MEDITATION?

Several suggestions have been made as to the derivation of the word 'meditation', one of these is from the Latin *meditari* which has been translated as meaning 'frequent', implying that it is a practice that should be performed regularly.[2] It may also stem from another Latin word *mederi* which has been translated as 'to attend to'.[3] From the literature it can be seen that meditation is an umbrella term for a widely disparate collection of activities and techniques. Every different school or tradition of meditation gives a slightly different definition of what it actually means to them, although one can begin to extract a common thread running through the various descriptions. Common to all sitting meditations is a turning of the attention inwards, a quieting of the mind, by focusing the attention on the movement of the breath, or by reciting a word or phrase (mantra).

The conscious everyday mind is effectively 'bypassed', and one learns to be aware of the perpetual stream of thoughts that course through our heads unbidden, and see the extent to which they usually control us without our conscious knowledge. One of the goals of meditation is to go beyond these restless distractions and relax in that place which Thomas Merton refers to as 'beyond thought and concept, a place of direct awareness'.[4] However it is perhaps more helpful to see meditation as a *process* rather than a goal. It is not so much a striving towards some prescribed end state, but more of a conscious practising to be totally *present* in a particular moment.

A valuable and succinct working definition has been given by West:

Thus meditation can be defined as an exercise in which the individual turns attention or awareness to dwell upon a single object, concept, sound, image or experience, with the intention of gaining greater spiritual or experiential or existential insight, or of achieving improved psychological well being.[5]

The two intentions of practising meditation highlighted in this definition can therefore be seen as *gaining greater spiritual insight* and *improved psychological well-being*. This echoes the historical progression of the purpose of meditation practices that I will describe next.

WHAT ARE THE DIFFERENT PURPOSES OF MEDITATION?

In order to disentangle the vast array of definitions and techniques listed under the general term of meditation, it is perhaps useful to take a historical perspective in which two distinct trends emerge.

(1) *The original spiritual purpose*: on the one hand, the rich spiritual legacy can be traced back over 2,500 years, where it can be seen that meditative techniques and practices are at the heart of every great religious tradition. They have been used as tools to attain spiritual development and the means of attaining special kinds of awareness and the highest states of consciousness that man is capable of.[6] Meditation is often thought of as an Eastern phenomenon at the heart of Hindu and Buddhist traditions as well as Sikhism, Taoism, Judaism and the Sufi sects of Islam. What is not so well known is that meditational practices have also long been part of the Western religious life stemming from the fourth-century Christian Hesychastic practices of the desert fathers in Egypt.[7] Their meditation practices and rules for living had striking parallels with Hinduism and Buddhism and have strongly influenced Christian monasticism to the present day.

The purpose of these practices was to facilitate greater spiritual or existential insight by developing the power of concentration. The power or strength of mind which arises when the mind is unified and brought to one-pointedness through concentration on a stimulus. They were primarily intended for religious initiates and devout lay people. An exception was the first stage of Zen Buddhism or *Bompu* Zen which was designed for anyone who desired to practice, because it was free of philosophic or religious content. It was practised in the belief that it could improve *physical and mental health*. This leads one to the growing contemporary reason for meditating that has little to do with spirituality and everything to do with psychological well-being.

(2) *The contemporary secular purpose*: on the other hand, a more recent phenomenon is the extraction of meditation from its religious connotations and its use as a secular, therapeutic device in the West to relieve distress or to improve psychological well-being. This can be seen in the meditation practice of Transcendental Meditation which was adapted for Western use from ancient Indian techniques in the 1960s, and which excited the interest of scientists, resulting in a proliferation of research projects attempting to analyse the phenomenon in great detail. Other secular meditation practices include Carrington's Clinically Standardized Meditation,[8] Benson's Method[9] and Buddhist 'Mindfulness' meditation, among others. All of these are fully described in the literature, and can be employed as practical techniques to

train the mind in concentration to achieve psychological and physical well-being. It is this area of improving psychological well-being that I see as the most important for children's education.

RESEARCH INTO THE EFFECTS OF MEDITATION

Up until now the interest in meditation has mainly centred around its use by adults. The literature exhaustively documents the research on the claimed benefits of practising meditation. In order to see the potential of meditation for use in education, it is important to touch on the physiological and psychological benefits that have been attributed to its use. In other words, what actually happens in the mind and the body during and as an effect of meditation? Murphy[10] summarized 1,300 studies which alluded to the inter-related benefits of meditation and they can briefly be divided into:

(1) *Physiological benefits*: lowered heart rate; reduced blood pressure; reduced anxiety; relaxed muscles; improved motor skills; alleviated pain; reversed heart disease; and alleviation of drug dependency, among many other things.
(2) *Psychological benefits*: increased empathy; heightened perception; heightened auditory acuity; improved memory; increased clarity of thought; increased creativity; improved self-confidence and self-discipline, among many other side effects.

Of the many benefits claimed, there is increasingly convincing evidence for positive physiological and psychological effects ensuing from the practice of meditation, and it is possible to highlight a few that could be beneficial to education.

WHAT EFFECTS OF MEDITATION COULD BE USEFUL IN EDUCATION?

Stress management
Researchers consider meditation to be a 'unique physiological state',[11] which is different from both sleep and ordinary wakefulness, although sharing some of the attributes of each. During meditation the body enters a profound state of relaxation such as is experienced during the deepest stages of sleep, while being at the same time alert and wakeful. It is a state that can counterbalance the negative effects of stress and be highly beneficial.

'Whole brained' functioning
During meditation, researchers of Transcendental Meditation have referred to the occurrence of 'hypersynchrony' of the brain waves, where the density of alpha brain waves (peaceful and rythmic) increase in both hemispheres of the brain. This usually only happens when one is asleep. During meditation, synchrony between the two hemispheres means that the brain retains clarity and alertness without going to sleep. The most important fact is not that there is one specific brain wave or pattern of waves, but the 'unusual evenness and rhythmicity of whichever wave is occurring' which produced the tendency of all the areas to 'harmonize and pulsate together'.[12] Much has been talked in

recent years, about left and right brained thinking styles, and it is now acknowledged that the highest achievements of science and art have required a synthesis of the functioning of both sides of the brain. Meditation therefore can produce a relaxed yet alert functioning of the brain which is the state required for optimum, effective learning, of which more will be discussed in Chapter 8.

Training attention

The processes of learning how to 'wake up', or to pay attention to the present moment are central to any understanding of meditation. At its most essential, meditation is the art of learning to pay attention.

No educationalist would deny that concentration is a central prerequisite for optimum efficient and effective learning. Children in school are constantly exhorted to 'pay attention' and to 'concentrate' on the task in hand, without ever being specifically taught how to do it. Attention entails remaining focused on and consciously aware of what one is doing. The Oxford Dictionary defines *attention* as: 'the act or faculty of applying one's mind; consideration; care; erect attitude of readiness'. A word that is linked to attention is *concentration*. Here the dictionary states: 'to concentrate is to employ ones full thoughts or efforts; bring together at one point; mental faculty of exclusive attention'.

Focus: it has been suggested[13] that attention is multi-dimensional and runs along a continuum from tight or 'spotlight' focus to broad or 'floodlight' focus. The whole spectrum of attention is necessary at different times in learning. A good learner will learn to vary the direction and quality of attention for maximum appropriateness to the task in hand.

Absorption: at its most concentrated and absorbed state, attention has been called the 'Flow',[14] 'Peak Experiences',[15] 'the Meditative mood',[16] or 'the Zone' in the sporting world. It is a state in which individuals become totally absorbed in what they are doing and can lose track of time. The essence of 'flow' is a highly concentrated mental state focused on the task in hand where the mind and body work effortlessly and pleasurably as one. It has now been demonstrated[17] that the 'Flow' state is a prerequisite for optimum learning. Meditation as a discipline can be an effective way of developing this elusive, spontaneous process into a formal practice.

LEARNING TO BE IN THE PRESENT MOMENT

Meditation is essentially the process of training the mind in attention to the present moment. It provides exercises in quieting the conscious cognitive processes that Eastern religions have referred to as the 'chattering monkey', or the 'ego chatter'. It allows one to be aware of the extent to which we have little control over our thoughts as we function on 'automatic pilot', reacting unconsciously to events and our perception of them. Normally thoughts and 'ego chatter' form a barrier to the world and one's experience of it, and one walks through life like a sleep walker. Every great religion has discovered and taught ways to sidestep the automatic reflexes and conditioned responses of the human mind, in order to see the world in its pristine state, free of preconceptions. As Kafka famously suggested: 'We see things not as they are but as we are'. Through the process of meditation one becomes alert to the hitherto unconscious stream of commentary and judgements that the mind is prone to, over which one initially has alarmingly little control. Teaching children to 'wake up' to every moment could have revolutionary repercussions for the quality of their engagement in learning.

CONCLUSION

This chapter has attempted to explore what meditation actually is while, at the same time, being wary of the very process of crystallizing it into a set definition. A distinction has been made between the historical heritage of meditation at the heart of all the great religions, and the contemporary phenomenon of extracting it from these religious roots and using it as a secular practice to enhance physiological and psychological well-being. There have been strong claims and some research evidence to show that meditation can affect mental, physical and emotional states. The main areas where meditation can be seen as beneficial in education were explored, namely: stress management; achieving a relaxed yet alert mental state; training attention and concentration and being in the present moment. There would seem to be a good case for exploring these attributes of mind in education where these psychological states would appear to be at a premium.

It is strange how little attention education pays to the state of mind and the psychological functioning of the learner. Giving children the tools to be in the optimal state for learning would seem to be a good idea. As we have seen the words 'pay attention' are a phrase that is reiterated to children in school perhaps more regularly than any other. Meditation is first and foremost a technique to cultivate attention. For something that is so obviously deemed important for learning as well as for life, it is surprising that the art of paying attention is a subject that never appears on the curriculum.

The practical implications of these states of mind have been explored in the recent research that I have been carrying out as part of my M.Ed. and Ph.D. degrees into the role that meditation can play in effective lifelong learning. A section of this research and a concentration meditation exercise will be described in Chapter 8.

NOTES

1 Fontana, D. and Slack, I. (1997) *Teaching Meditation to Children.* Shaftesbury: Element Books; Rozen, D. (1975) *Meditating with Children.* Boulder Creek, Calif.: Planetary Publications.

2 Fontana, D. (1991) *The Elements of Meditation.* Shaftesbury: Element Books.

3 Simon, M. (1993) *Born Contemplative.* London: Darton, Longman & Todd.

4 Merton, T. (1959) quoted in Miller, J. P. (1994) *The Contemplative Practitioner: Meditation in Education and the Professions.* London: Beign & Garvey, p. 27.

5 West, M. (ed.) (1987) *The Psychology of Meditation.* Oxford: Clarendon Press, p. 10.

6 Carrington, P. (1998) *The Book of Meditation: The Complete Guide to Modern Meditation.* Shaftesbury: Element Books.

7 Goleman, D. (1988) *The Meditative Mind*. Los Angeles: J. P. Tarcher, p. 55.
8 Carrington, P. (1977) *Freedom in Meditation*. Garden City, NY: Anchor Press.
9 Benson, H. (1975) *The Relaxation Response*. New York: Avon Books.
10 Murphy, M. and Donovan, S. (1997) *The Physical and Psychological Effects of Meditation*. Sausalito, Calif: Institute of Noetic Sciences.
11 Carrington, *Freedom in Meditation*, p. 55.
12 Carrington, ibid., p. 47.
13 Claxton, G. (1999) *Wise Up: The Challenge of Lifelong Learning*. London: Bloomsbury.
14 Csikszentmihalyi, M. (1990) *Flow: The Psychology of Optimal Experience*. New York: Harper & Row.
15 Maslow, A. (1962) *Towards a Psychology of Being*. New York: Van Nostrand Reinhold.
16 Carrington, ibid.
17 Goleman, D. (1995) *Emotional Intelligence*. New York: Bantam, p. 93.

CHAPTER 8

Meditation and the process of learning

Caroline Mann

INTRODUCTION

There is growing anxiety about the quality of learning in our schools, despite a decade of exhaustive reforms in education. Nixon *et al.*[1] point out that there is a growing realization that the agenda of the recent past has failed to address the continuing levels of underachievement in our schools. The present government has pledged to raise educational standards as its main priority, under the battle cry of 'education, education, education'. However the quality of the future of education depends *not* on the quantitative expansion of access and availability of education, as is commonly thought, but on a transformation of the way individuals think of themselves as *learners* and an awareness that certain mental and emotional prerequisites (or 'scaffolding') need to be in place before real learning can occur. Many children are disenchanted by schools because they have come to see themselves as incapable of handling academic work and feel that the curriculum is not relevant to life outside school. They are not receptive to learning because of the negative perceptions they hold of themselves as individuals and as learners. The questions that need to be asked are not how many subjects can we cram into a school day, but what is the motivation and mental/emotional state of the learner? Can children be taught to shift their capacity to learn?

The conventional notion of intelligence as a fixed ability has been overturned in the last 20 years. The dramatic increase in our knowledge of the workings of our brains has been facilitated by neuroscience using revolutionary new computerized techniques to explore the living brain in action.[2] This has led to a flourishing of interest in 'learning how to learn' and the awareness that humans have the capacity to enhance the intelligence they inherited.[3] This was further illuminated by the convincing suggestion that we have many different types of intelligence.[4] In this chapter, I would like to outline a section of my Ph.D. research project on the effect of meditation on learning in order to propose a qualitative change in the way we view the learning process.

A RESEARCH PROJECT: THE EFFECT OF MEDITATION ON ATTENTION AND CONCENTRATION

Certain prerequisites must be in place before meaningful learning can occur. For different reasons, children only take in a small percentage of the material that is presented to them,[5] which renders much learning that is done in schools and elsewhere highly inefficient. However exciting the contents of a lesson or however dynamic the teacher is at presenting the material (although these help), little will be learned unless the pupil is fully present, not just physically, but both mentally and emotionally as well. In Chapter 7, I outlined what I felt to be the essential contribution that meditation could have on learning by affecting the psychological state of mind of the learner specifically by training attention and concentration. Some questions that I set out to answer in the research were whether a normal group of children in an ordinary school could be taught to meditate. Could this training in attention have an effect by making them more mentally and emotional present? I took a group of 12–13-year-old children in a local comprehensive to train them in certain meditation techniques over an eleven-week period. A class in the same year acted as the control group. Before and after the course the groups were measured in certain mental and emotional areas to attempt to see if there had been any effect from the meditation.

The emotional states considered relevant to learning that I chose to address were: self-esteem; locus of control; stress and anxiety. The mental attributes chosen were intelligence and memory. All of them were felt to be prerequisites to effective lifelong learning. The research used a combination of qualitative and quantitative methods of data collection. The quantitative methods were seen in the longitudinal measuring scales employed to measure any changes in the children in these five areas, before and after the eleven-week course. There were also three cross-sectional experiments in the form of memory games devised for use within a lesson on a particular day, one of these will be described later on in this chapter. The qualitative methods were seen in a variety of interviews, questionnaires and diaries with the children and their staff.

WHAT FORM OF INTERVENTION WAS USED?

The intervention in this research case study took the form of a eleven-week course in meditation with the selected tutor group. I fully realized that for use in a school setting the meditation technique needed be free of any specific religious denomination, connotation or proprietary brand name, in order to be accepted by the majority of parents, teachers and children. The meditation I finally devised was based on the key denominators common to most sitting meditation practices in the literature, namely: physical relaxation and training the mind in attention by focusing on a stimulus.

Preparation for meditation
Posture
It is very important to sit with your back straight and preferably not resting on the back of the chair. Imagine that an invisible thread is attached lightly to the top of your head, and gently pulls you up straight. If sitting on a chair your feet should be flat on the floor and not

crossed. Try and make sure that your head is upright, and your arms hang loosely by your sides, with your hands gently resting on your lap. Let your eyes look down at the floor in front of you and then let them close. If this feels strange at first, you can open them whenever you need to, but try to keep your gaze down at the floor to avoid being distracted. You will soon get used to keeping them closed all the time.

Physical relaxation exercises (these can be varied)

Imagine that you are sitting under a warm waterfall of water, that is washing away any tensions and tiredness as it flows over you. Put your attention on the top of your head and consciously relax the muscles of your scalp, face and neck. Feel the warm water splash over your head and face. Then move your shoulders gently in a circle backwards and then forwards to release the tensions that can build up in this area. Feel the water splash over your shoulders. Feel your arms hanging loosely by your side and your hands folded gently on your lap. Allow your attention to go down your body, relaxing the muscles consciously as you go. Down your back and then your front. Feel the chair under you as you sit firmly on it. Let your attention go down each leg in turn, feeling the bend at the knee and the ankle. Feel your feet resting on the floor, and give your toes a wiggle to release any tensions. Feel the water flow all over you taking the tensions and tiredness away from you.

Deep Breathing

This is harder to do than you might imagine at first! Usually we only breathe using the top part of our lungs, leaving all the stale air at the bottom untouched. This breathing is going to use the whole of your lungs. Take a deep breath slowly in through your nose as you count to three, then hold the breath for the count of one, then SLOWLY let the air out through your mouth as you count to three. Feel the air go deep down in your lungs until the ribcage is fully extended. Be careful not to let your shoulders rise up, nothing should move except your ribcage and stomach, swelling as the air goes in and deflating as the air is expelled. You can imagine a balloon inside your stomach that you want to blow up with air. Imagine what colour it is and feel it grow full and round as the air is breathed into it. Gradually as you get better you can extend the deep breathing from this 3:1:3 breathing to 7:1:7 counts. Breathing in through the nose for the count of 7, hold for one count and breathe the air out, really slowly and silently, for the count of 7, through the mouth. At first it may not seem possible to hold the breath for so long, but soon it will become second nature to you. Now breathe normally.

Thoughts and distractions

During the meditation you will be aware of thoughts from time to time. Our minds often daydream without us being aware of it. When you become aware that you are thinking, don't push the thoughts away roughly, but allow them to drift away gently, like clouds in a summer sky. Return your attention to your breathing. There may be distracting noises as well; in the same way, notice the sound and let it go and return your attention to the breathing. Do you hear an individual sound or are all the sounds merging into a symphony of sound? The mind is used to 'catching' distracting thoughts and noises and 'playing' with them. Get used to just being aware of them but not attaching any importance or meaning to them. Just let them go. There is no competition and no prizes. Come back each time to the breathing.

The meditation
Watching the breath

Let your mind go into 'soft focus' and turn your attention inwards. Be aware of the beat of your heart and any internal sensations. Become aware of your breathing, not the deep breathing that you did before, but gentle, soft breathing. Put your attention on the tip of your nose, and watch the breath as it enters and leaves the nostrils. Rather like a guard on duty at the gate of a city, watching the people coming in and out. Notice the exact moment when the in-breath becomes the out-breath. Watch the breath in this way for a bit. (With a class of children being led through the meditation, I would count out loud, softly and very slowly, to 20 while they do this, to give them a reference point for concentration.)

Concentrating on the breath with a mantra (word)
Now take your attention down into the centre of your chest. Gently breath in, and as you breath *out*, silently say the word 'CALM' to yourself. You could choose a word or phrase of your own to say here if you prefer. Any word or phrase that has a special meaning for you, and is not used much in normal conversation. BREATH IN, BREATH OUT, 'CALM' etc. Breathe in and out gently in this way, letting the word or phrase resonate inside you as you breathe out. Let the sound do what it wants to, sometimes being soft and quiet, sometimes fading out altogether, and sometimes sounding loud. Carry on doing this for some minutes. (I count out loud softly to 30 while they do this.) When you are ready, open your eyes.

THE EFFECT ON COGNITIVE CAPACITY

In this chapter there is only time to briefly mention the research area of cognitive capacity. This was measured in two ways: by the Ravens Matrices and by three memory experiments.

1. *The Ravens Progressive Matrices Scale.*[6] This scale was selected as the most suitable indicator of intelligence that is readily available to a teacher. Although it only measures performance intelligence, and must be seen in relation to the verbal intelligence to give a full intelligence score, the Ravens gives an indication of cognitive ability for the purposes of research. This scale was used longitudinally, both before and after the eleven weeks, with the research group and the control group, in order to see if there was any change in cognitive functioning. The mean average of the research group's IQ scores went up from 100.86 before the course, to 105.91 after the course in meditation, which was statistically significant. Thirteen children had increased in IQ, while seven had decreased and three remained the same. The minimum-maximum scores before and after the course also showed a shift up of IQs with the before scores being 80–125 (with one child having 125), to 93–125 afterwards (with two children now having a score of 125). This did not occur in the control group, where their IQ scores were seen on average to decrease.

It was not the intention of the research to assert whether or not the children had actually increased in intelligence. What was proposed was that the meditation had trained the class to concentrate and be more fully present while the tests were in progress. The effect of this increased engagement was to clear the 'cognitive static' and 'inoculate' the class from distractions, thereby enabling them to function to the best of their ability.

2. *The Cross Sectional Memory Games.* I devised three memory games that were used before and after a meditation in a single lesson, and aimed at measuring the effect of meditation on the recall of information. Once again, because of space, I can only describe one: The Kim's Memory Game. This game was adapted from the well-known children's game first detailed in *Kim* by Rudyard Kipling. In the game the children were shown twenty ordinary household objects in turn out of a bag. They were then hidden from view and the children had four minutes to write down as many objects as they could remember. The research group then had a 15–20 minute meditation while the control group had an ordinary lesson. At the end of this time they had another four minutes to write down as many of the objects as they could remember, *without* being shown the items again.

It would be natural to assume that the class would remember more immediately after being shown the objects. However, the research group, on average, remembered more objects after the twenty minute meditation, with their mean average scores rising from 12.11 to 16.05 (out of 20). The control group remembered on average much less the second time. This proved to be a statistically significant result. This little experiment gave the most conclusive evidence that meditation has a profound effect on the ability to recall information.

The children remarked on the effect meditation had on their minds and bodies: 'After meditating my whole body feels refreshed and my mind is clear'; another said 'It is calming and relaxing and best of all, it clears my mind'. Yet another said that meditation helped him remember more 'because it makes more space in my brain'. Because meditation is essentially a subjective experience it is hard to express what it feels like. One boy summed this up:

> 'It is an experience that is almost impossible to put into words. However, the closest I can get is that it is like diving into the sea.'

CONCLUSION

The findings of the research suggested that profound positive changes occurred in the cognitive capacity of the children due to the meditation process. Training the mind in the art of attention/concentration would seem to lead to a shift in the quality of engagement in the learning process, and therefore a shift in the capacity to learn. Learning to be emotionally and mentally present could be seen as providing the prerequisite 'platform' for learning to take place. This would seem to have significant implications for the future of effective lifelong learning.

A long time ago Pythagoras put it like this: 'Learn to be silent. Let your quiet mind listen and absorb.'

NOTES

1   Nixon, J. *et al.* (1996) *Encouraging Learning: Towards a Theory of the Learning School.* Buckingham: Open University Press.
2   Greenfield, S. (1995) *Journey to the Centre of the Mind.* New York: W. H. Freeman; Greenfield, S. (1997) *The Human Brain: A Guided Tour.* London: Weidenfeld & Nicolson.
3   Blagg, N. (1991) *Can we Teach Intelligence?* Hillside, New Jersey: Laurence Erlbaum; Fisher, R. (1990) *Teaching Children to Think.* Hemel Hempstead: Simon & Schuster; Jenson, E. (1994) *The Learning Brain.* San Diego, Calif.: Turning Point Publishers; Dryden, Gordon and Vos, Jeanette (1994) *The Learning Revolution.* Aylesbury, Bucks: Accelerated Learning Systems; Sharron, H. (1994) *Changing Children's Minds.* Birmingham: Sharron Publishing; Rose, C. (1985) *Accelerated Learning.* Aylesbury, Bucks: Accelerated Learning Systems Ltd.
4   Gardner, H. (1983) *Frames of Mind: A Theory of Multiple Intelligences.* New York: Basic Books.
5   Fontana, D. and Slack, I. (1997) *Teaching Meditation to Children.* Shaftesbury: Element Books.
6   Ravens, J. C. (1965) *The Guide to the Standard Progressive Matrices.* London: H. K. Lewis.

CHAPTER 9

Meditation in teacher education: towards teachers as practitioners

Clive Erricker

It is now explicitly stated within the 1988 Education Reform Act that one of the main aims of education that underpins and is addressed within curriculum learning is the promotion of pupils' spiritual, moral, social and cultural development.[1] This sits alongside their mental and physical development. The purpose of this chapter is to show how meditation can contribute to these aims when considering teacher education.

EXPERIENTIAL LEARNING AND MEDITATION[2]

Often, students who embark on a BA(QTS), or B.Ed. degree, or onto a PGCE, already have had educational experiences and a broader socialization that militates against experiential learning, within which I subsume meditation. Experiential learning is a way of learning through reflection on one's own experience, and an interpretation and communication of the same. Its great benefit is that the reflection and communication that ensue involve not only rational reflection but attention given to what one feels, affective learning or emotional literacy, and the will, what one desires, and what one understands as just, right and true. In other words, one speaks from one's whole worldview and the responses and discussion that ensue have depth, really matter and become part of a community understanding. This also involves trust, and therefore risk, and listening carefully with the head and the heart. This is very different to just learning a curriculum, gaining academic knowledge, or developing specific skills in relation to competencies identified. Nevertheless, it underpins all of these.

Meditation is a way of coming to know yourself and of observing yourself, and the world you participate in, mindfully; that is with full attention. It is also a way of reflecting on your experience dispassionately and, as a result, acquiring knowledge. Thus, it has an obvious role within experiential learning and education generally. Nevertheless, as indicated above, this is little understood, if at all, by those who embark on a teacher training programme.

An added frustration can be that such programmes are intense in relation to the amount of time spent on curriculum learning and the expectations required in other areas, including teaching practice. There is little time to reflect outside the classroom, whether in the college or university or the school. There is also an economy required in relation to delivery, by the subject specialist lecturer in the higher education institution, and by the trainee teacher in the school placement. Further, the imposition of prescription by the Teacher Training Agency (TTA), and standards and inspection by the Office for Standards in Education (Ofsted), do not encourage experimentation or the inclusion of modes of learning that have broader aims, 'fuzzier' outcomes and take more time.

If we put all these restrictions together it is easy to see why experiential learning generally, and meditation in particular, are viewed with some suspicion by those with no prior commitment to their educational efficacy.

My own specialist teaching area is religious education. Although this is a discrete subject, I understand it as being embedded in education as a whole. Therefore, anything I teach must serve wider educational aims as well as those relating directly to the subject. In doing this I am bearing in mind that education is a vehicle or a tool which serves people's growth. When it ceases to do this it is not useful. I understand religion in the same way. This means I cannot teach about religions as abstract entities, I must keep in mind that religions are the expression of people's faiths and beliefs. They are intimately related to people's experiences and influence the way those experiences are understood. This leads on to the recognition that there is an interrelationship between religion, culture and people's enculturation or socialization. The outcome of this is that I must understand my teaching and my students' learning as caught up within, and a part of, an organic and complex process of change. That makes it education. The important question then becomes 'How does it influence this process, how does it lead to growth?'

EMPOWERING LEARNING

Here I follow certain criteria as a means of creating a process which we can call learning or development, but the terms are hardly adequate. First, I wish to encourage my students to gain ownership of their own transformation. If they resist this process they will not, as a result, resist change. Change will occur as they move from being students to becoming teachers, but they will be passive inheritors of it. They will be waiting to be told what to do and how to do it. Thus, this will be the basis of their own teaching. In other words they will be bad teachers because they will not encourage growth in their own pupils; they will just instil and measure competencies.

Second, to gain ownership of their own transformation, they must be aware of themselves as actors, as people who already own stories, or identities, and express these stories in their communication with themselves and others. This means they must be reflexive or aware of their role in the teaching and learning situation, what they bring to that role, what they take away from it, and what part they play in it. If this does not happen they will see the situation as one in which others act but they 'neutrally' or 'objectively' observe, participate, or instruct.

This is an equivalent of a pre-Copernican view of the universe, psychologically translated. Each individual thinks of him or herself as the fixed centre round which others revolve and the views, activities and values of others are subjected to the normality of judgement of that individual. Thus the 'pre-Copernican' individual is immutable and psychologically justified in being so since they are the fixed centre. It is easy to see how this then translates into a view of 'others' as strange, wrong, or even employs the last protective device of one who does not wish to engage – 'well you have your view and I have mine'. The unstated supposition here is that 'I am right and you are wrong, but you just can't see that'. Such a psychological attitude cannot produce a good teacher.

Third, in order to overcome the above situation, I have to ask individuals to disclose their stories or narratives within the group. This can be uncomfortable as we move from a solely 'rational' idea of learning to the inclusion of a more affective one. Here I must encourage these responses through specific strategies. The key to this is understanding how we express our stories, both to ourselves and in relating to others. We do so through telling orally and ritually, in gesture and touch. This telling reveals a world that works on a symbolic, non-literal, metaphoric level of relationship. Thus, a symbolic object is no longer an object at all but a representation of something non-material to which it points. It is an image. This is true whether the object has religious or non-religious significance.

We may start with an object we are wearing or carry about with us. We may bring objects in. Discussion can be lighthearted or serious. We can move between the two and notice that humour and seriousness are not two unrelated qualities, but often intimately related to each other. A story that begins with a 19-year-old's teddy bear can move on to the importance of a relationship with a grandparent. A football can be the means of telling of a relationship with a father. At this point transformation is already occurring as we listen carefully to the narratives of others, recognize their distinctiveness, but are reminded of buried ones of our own that are suddenly brought to mind. We start to understand the construction of people's narratives, the value that they have, and the 'normality' of diversity. We can move on to where these objects are kept and why they are kept there. This introduces us to the non-literal or metaphoric geography of space – why we arrange our environment as we do, relationally as well as for practical purposes.

Fourth, we can start to understand space differently. Space is a positive thing within which we place or find things. This is as true for the space within which thoughts and feelings occur as it is for the space within which we arrange objects: our bedroom or our classroom. The two types of space are connected by association. The 'outer space' affects the 'inner space' and vice versa.

Fifth, we can move on to silence as a type of space within which sounds and thoughts happen. The question is 'What do we want to do with this space?' This necessarily leads us into meditation. Meditation is simply enquiring into this silence to gain ownership of it, to understand what occupies it and how that affects the way we think and act, the opinions we voice and call our own, the effect of moods and emotions on this, and how all these things arise and fade. We are back to change and how we deal with change.

Here are two meditations I do with students to introduce mindfulness and focus the attention.

Enquiring into silence

Sitting silently and following the movement of the breath with your attention, close your eyes. Notice anything that arises: sounds, physical sensations, thoughts and feelings. Notice them arising in your mind and let them pass through. Pay attention simply to what arises as though the mind is a detector of activity but stores nothing. As you do this notice the space and silence that increases as the mind relaxes. Let this happen for a few minutes.

Doing what you enjoy

Now turn your attention to an activity you enjoy. Follow it through in detail, as though your mind is a camera recording in slow motion. Feel the flow of the activity and be with it as though you were doing it now. Be with the activity and forgetful of the self. Then turn your attention to the feelings arising as you do this and relax into them.

After doing these two meditations reflect on the changes that occurred and how these came about.

The following quotations fit well with these two meditations.

'Oh, how freely come and go the myriad forms of things!' (Han Shan[3])
   'The first step in growth is to do what we love to do and to become aware of doing it.' (Sujata[4])

CHILDREN AS ARTISTS OF THEIR OWN LIVES

If we think that we can accomplish all this because we are intelligent, grown up individuals we need to be disabused of such an idea. One way to do this is to listen to or read children's narratives and see the same process occurring there that we have been through. In the following extracts from her story, a 9-year-old girl relates her experience of her parents separating and certain ways in which she has dealt with that. Look for the way in which space and objects become significant in relation to her relationships, experiences and emotions, how she uses language to communicate her story, and how she deals with this situation and its anxieties. Without being introduced to meditation she naturally inclines to finding space away from her situation in which she experiences tranquillity and reassurance.

M: When I first came into year five it's been quite a while since my dad left home, 'cos my mum and dad are separated, but sometimes my mum finds it hard to give us money and that and then my sister started going to school and throwing tantrums at school 'cos she didn't want to go and that ... well, I can't always do it but normally me and my mum row ... when I get back from my dad's or something. I go to my dad's nearly every day and I go to my dad's and it's mine and my step-brother's den and we go there and there's like this big bush with trees in where you can go and sit and then my dad, I think my dad knows about it but he doesn't know where it is, there's like ponies in the opposite field and if you climb over the fence ... there's a little stream that runs through and you can go over the bridges and it's like a never-ending depth ... and it's like really peaceful and it helps you calm down.

> ... sometimes, we all went out to the beach when I was first told about, I was playing on the beach with my sister and my mum goes, 'I've got something to tell you' and I was really happy and then when she said that dad was going away I thought then that he wasn't going to be my dad any more, 'cos the immediate reaction is, if he's going, who's going to be my dad? You don't think, yeh, but he's still gonna be my dad, but he's not going to be with me, you don't think that at first, you think that yeh, he's going, who's gonna take care of us?
>
> ... I've got another sort of den ... 'cos my dad can fix guns so he has to go up when they do bomb raids in Bosnia and that, in case they need any guns, and I get really worried that he's gonna get hurt or something, 'cos he's got a problem with his lungs and kidneys 'cos of his smoking and I get worried that he's gonna have a stroke or something and he's not gonna have his ID... cards and so if you really squeeze under it gets really dark and stuffy, but if you really, if I really miss him I try and snuggle under with some pillows and it just like makes me think of my dad, it just reassures me that he's gonna be okay. He did get ill and he's coming out of hospital tomorrow.

There is no fundamental difference in the process that occurs with adults and that which occurs with children. The only difference is that we are now aware of it, in a reflexive way. We can observe it and start to understand and use it appropriately in our professional role, in a way that helps our pupils. The value of meditation in this process is that it helps us 'unclutter' our mental space and gives us the opportunity to reassess situations by letting go of stress and anxiety. Thus we can act more positively and creatively. Put succinctly, this could be termed becoming artists of our own lives.[6] Other words for that are growth, education, change, transformation and empowerment. This is what I want my own students to achieve so that they can help their pupils achieve it.

NOTES

1 DFEE (1994) *Circular 1/94*. London: HMSO.
2 The most useful book on experiential learning, related to religious education but valuable in any educational context, is Hammond, J., Hay, D., Moxon, J., Netto, B., Raban, K., Straugheir, G. and Williams, C. (1990) *New Methods in Religious Education: An Experiential Approach*. London: Oliver and Boyd/Longman. It contains a wide range of activities.
3 Levey, J. (1987) *The Fine Arts of Relaxation, Concentration and Meditation: Ancient Skills for Modern Minds*. London: Wisdom Publications, p. 82.
4 Levey, ibid., p. 102. Joel Levey's book offers a wide range of meditational exercises like those used here, but in a more extended form.
5 A phrase used by the French philosopher and historian Michel Foucault.

CHAPTER 10

Meditation in religion and meditation in education

Clive Erricker

SUSPICION OF RELIGION

Religion, for those who are not religious, is often a daunting and uncomfortable word. After all aren't religious people those who want to sell something, take control and rid us of our freedom to think and do as we please? Religions sell ideologies in order, so we are told, to save our souls. Well whose soul is it anyway and who decides whether I have a soul to save apart from me? Yes, there is a clash between secular values and religious tradition which can suggest that religion should not be allowed to have any part in the shaping of education. But it takes little enquiry, if one can be motivated to undertake it, in order to show that the plural character of religions and each religion, and the plural character of the non-religious world, undermines this apparently straightforward understanding. It cannot be denied that religious ideologies are culpable for their share of spiritual and moral human damage, but so are all ideologies. Beneath the vociferous ideological surface of life there are stiller waters and qualities of insight, compassion, friendship and kindness upon which we rely for survival and growth. These can emerge from both religious and non-religious sources. Meditation, in its various forms, is a tool or a term for the cultivation of these qualities.

A second misconception surrounds the idea that meditation is about doing nothing, cutting oneself off from the world and seeking one's own salvation or peace. Of course, selfish motivations are present everywhere but such a view tends to be generated by wilful ignorance; aversion to that which is strange and which might actually change one into something other than what you are. This suspicion of the power and influence of meditation, as though it were a force that might take over, or a dangerous thing to dabble in, is similar to many erroneous views one heard about computers thirty years ago. Meditation and computers have this in common: they are both tools that can be helpful to us. The government seems to have recognized this very swiftly with regard to computers, since computer literacy is now one of the main aims of education, and many children are now far more advanced in this respect than their parents (alas this is the case with me). If only we would wake up to the fact that meditation is just as necessary a part of education as using computers. I look forward to the day when children come home to teach their parents how to use meditation as well as how to use the computer.

As someone whose professional life has been taken up with the study of religion and the desire to convince people that religious education matters as education, if it is approached appropriately, I can say (hopefully) I know a religious megalomaniac when I see one. On the other hand you also come to discern teachings and practices that are helpful within and beyond religious frameworks of meaning. Meditation is concerned with just these things. The acid test is who has control. If you have the authority and experience is the test of the value of a practice then only a lack of confidence or a misplaced sense of pride gets in the way. Simplicity is the essence of meditation and happiness is its aim. Two teachers, one religious in the conventional sense and one not, describe it in the following terms:

> Try to be mindful and let things take their natural course. Then your mind will become still in any surroundings, like a clear forest pool. All kinds of wonderful, rare animals will come to drink at the pool, and you will clearly see the nature of all things. You will see many strange and wonderful things come and go, but you will be still. This is the happiness of the Buddha.[1]

> Meditation is not an escape from the world; it is not an isolating self-enclosing activity, but rather the comprehension of the world and its ways. The world has little to offer apart from food, clothes and shelter, and pleasure with its great sorrows.
> Meditation is wandering away from this world; one has to be a total outsider. Then the world has a meaning ... Then love is not pleasure. From this all action begins that is not the outcome of tension, contradiction, the search for self-fulfilment or the conceit of power.[2]

The above observations of Ajahn Chah and Jiddu Krishnamurti can help us forward in our investigation as to how meditation can be a useful tool in the enterprise of education.

EDUCATION FOR GROWTH

From a different perspective the first chief inspector for education, Edmond Holmes, wrote in 1911:

> The function of education is to foster growth. By some of my readers this statement will be regarded as a truism; by others as a challenge; by others, again, when they have realized its inner meaning, as a 'wicked heresy'. I will begin by assuming it is a truism and will then try to prove that it is true.[3]

Holmes' comments, effectively ignored over the best part of a century, reflect the larger horizon of what concerns the growth of a child in ways other than just the inculcation of certain skills and specific competencies. Holmes himself would not have had meditation in mind as a way to promote the growth he referred to. At that time it had not translated itself into a Western environment, let alone an educational one. Yet it serves his purposes admirably. Enquiry, reflection, autonomy, independence of mind; qualities he valued highly in the pursuit of an alternative educational vision, all of these are the fruits of meditative practice, and they are integral to a more holistic educational provision. But an holistic education depends on the teacher and student, of whatever age, acknowledging that they do not just converse across opinions and rational views, or subscribe to the idea that one has knowledge to impart which the other just receives; rather they let understanding emerge as a result of enquiry through awareness of what arises in experience. That is what meditation is.

Central to this enterprise is the quality of trust. In religion it is trust in the teacher that makes meditation valuable as a spiritual tool or process. You trust or have faith in the teacher knowing what he or she is doing and having your spiritual welfare and development at heart. It seems to me we can transpose just the same process into education and schooling, the difference being that the religious context is removed. It is not possible to do this if you conceive of education being knowledge led, in an academic sense. Then there would be a difference between a religious curriculum and a secular one. Although curricula are important in schools there is a tendency to place curriculum knowledge before the other more embracing aims of education. This is one reason why we seem to have lost our sense of what the overall purposes of education are – what it means to develop as people. This, of course, has a wider effect within societies as a whole, especially what we call 'Western society', which has been dominated by a rationalist and empiricist creed over the last 400 years and arguably longer. It has also been dominated by a desire for economic wealth during the same period.

When Holmes suggests 'growth' can be identified as a heresy within education, if its meaning is fully understood; so too has meditation or contemplation produced heretics within religious traditions: many Sufis and, within the Christian tradition, Meister Eckhart, St John of the Cross and others most obviously testify to this. Why should this be so? One reason is because the investigation of experience without ultimately relying on conceptual thinking thus challenges conceptual maps of reality. It challenges and undermines doctrines, whether religious or secular, that say this is how the world is, this is what we must do, and this is how we should behave. This challenge to authority comes from determining that there is higher authority, whether within one's own consciousness and conscience or beyond oneself, that cannot be denied. Meditative experience is a basis of that authority: a being true to oneself. Like Holmes' term 'growth' the phrase 'being true to oneself' is held in high esteem until its deeper meaning and implication are fully understood. Then terms like 'duty' replace it in public rhetoric as the highest virtue.

The purpose of this chapter has been to show that meditation can be used in religion *and* education without any cause for anxiety, just so long as we are interested in the development of young people as a prime motivation. If we can concur with the following sentiments, the first by the educationalist Bruno Bettelheim, the second by Joel Levey, then we can proceed to take on board the value of meditation in education.

Today, as in times past, the most important and also the most difficult task in raising a child is helping him or her to find meaning in life. Many growth experiences are needed to achieve this. The child, as he or she develops, must learn step by step to understand him or herself better; with this he or she becomes more able to understand others, and eventually can relate to them in ways which are mutually satisfying and meaningful.[4]

This book is for everyone interested in learning methods to master stress and enhance the quality of their life. It is also a handbook for those who wish to understand and master such skills in order to teach them to others. Whatever your motivation, you will find that the ideas and techniques in this collection have been presented with an emphasis on practical application in our modern lives, whilst preserving the sacredness of such inner arts of mental development. I suggest that you consider these ideas with your mind, sense their meaning for you in your heart, and test and confirm the power and practicality of these skills with your experience.[5]

DOING MEDITATION

To finish I should like to give an example of how one can take a meditative activity from its religious context and place it in an educational one.

The basis of this activity is observation, relaxation and awareness. We shall focus on a candle flame. Candles have symbolic significance within religions but are also usual household objects, often with romantic associations. They are used in both contexts and are therefore useful for this purpose. Symbolism, as a way of giving significance to something by prior association, is not intended here.

Looking at a candle flame, like looking into an open fire, is relaxing in itself. Observe the flame: just watch it and pay attention. Does it flicker, grow small and then larger? Does it dance from side to side? Observe it in detail, keep your attention on it and let it work on you. Notice the light in the flame and around the flame, note how the light fades away in the distance from the flame. Where does it meet the darkness or are there just changes in light? See the light and darkness as one. They meet each other and are within each other. Just observe this. Continue to watch as closely as you can. If the mind wanders bring its attention back to the flame...Close your eyes and see the flame in your mind, see it as clearly as you can using your concentration but not forcing, or using tension, or effort...As you open your eyes see the flame again, any smoke rising from it and the detail of what is in front of you. Stay with that for a few minutes. No hurry – nothing to do, nowhere to go. Be with the flame...Then ask yourself: who is watching, who is watching? Repeat your name and hear it sound in the silence. No you, just the flame, the sound and the silence. Close your eyes and gently, when you are ready, come out of the meditation.

If doing this activity reduces stress and tension, induces calm and self-forgetfulness and helps you to realize the potential effect of a simple meditational activity then you can see its value. If this gives you confidence, it is the first step to doing something similar with your students. Classrooms are such busy places with active minds going everywhere as we think, talk and enquire or fail to pay attention, that they can seem inhospitable to silence and contemplation. But that can be changed in just a few minutes once we have receptive minds.

Such activities as these can have powerful effects of association and we must be aware of that. Once, after doing this activity, a participant said that he saw his dead father when looking into the flame. To say that is to give something intimate and personal to the group you are with. This did not mean he was upset or that something had happened that was negative about which something had to be done, but it is a reminder to encourage a supportive environment in which we can work with ourselves and one another. To conclude, three words of advice I try to follow: be confident, be sensitive and take one step at a time. And three final quotes that can be related to the above meditation:

'Look lovingly on some object. Do not go on to another object. Here in the middle of this object – the blessing.'[6]

'Enter the sound of your own name and, through this sound, all sounds.'[7]

'See, as if for the first time, a beauteous person or an ordinary object.'[8]

NOTES

1 Chah, Ajahn (1975) *A Still Forest Pool*, in Jack Kornfield and Paul Breitner (eds.), New York: Quest, Preface.

2 Krishnamurti, J. (1973) *The Only Revolution*. Mary Lutyens (ed.), London: Gollancz, p. 9.

3 Shute, C. (1998) *Edmond Holmes and 'The Tragedy of Education'*. Nottingham: Educational Heretics Press, p. 5.

4 Bettelheim, B. (1991) *The Uses of Enchantment: The Meaning and Importance of Fairy Tales*. London: Penguin, p. 3.

5 Levey, J. (1987) *The Fine Arts of Relaxation, Concentration and Meditation: Ancient Skills for Modern Minds*. London: Wisdom Publications, p. 13.

6 Reps, P. (1982) 'Centring', in *Zen Flesh, Zen Bones*. Harmondsworth: Penguin, p. 156.

7 Ibid., p. 162.

8 Ibid., p. 158.

CHAPTER 11

Meditation and spiritual development

Clive Erricker

Without curiosity, without the inclination to question, and without the exercise of imagination, insight and intuition, young people would lack the motivation to learn and their intellectual development would be impaired. Deprived of self-understanding and, potentially, of the ability to understand others, they may experience difficulty in co-existing with neighbours and colleagues to the detriment of their social development. Were they not moved by feelings of awe and wonder at the beauty of the world we live in, or the power of artists, musicians and writers to manipulate space, sound and language, they would live in an inner cultural desert.[1]

HOW DOES MEDITATION CHANGE SPIRITUAL EDUCATION?

The above lyrical exhortation to attend to young people's spiritual development, aligned with their moral, social and cultural development, can be found at the beginning of the first official document that took it seriously. It comes from the National Curriculum Council's Discussion Paper in 1993. Later, in 1995, it was republished by the body that followed the NCC, the School Curriculum and Assessment Authority (SCAA). That, in turn, has now become the Quality Curriculum Authority (QCA). Within the documentation – reports, discussion papers and other guidance that has been produced within this transmutation – the word meditation appears only once.[2] Also, we may note that the tone of these documents changes and loses the expansive quality of the passage above, progressively preoccupying itself with children becoming more moral.[3] Even in the literature that has been produced by those researching, debating and seeking to guide provision for spiritual education there is scarcely a mention of meditation.[4] Why should this be so?

In part the problem lies with the idea that we must define 'spirituality'. Thus we see attempts to do this that relate it to religion, to the arts, to feelings and relationships, and to knowledge and learning.[5] But this attempt to treat spirituality as a thing has to be resisted; however, this creates difficulties. Our understanding of education substantially depends upon the idea that once we know what something is we can teach it and our students can learn it. If I can't define it or, at least, construct a curriculum (a body of knowledge) to teach from – what can I *do*? In my experience of working with teachers on post-Ofsted action plans and inset days this has been a genuine problem for them.

But the problem has a deeper source, as I now wish to argue. First, spiritual development is not gained through the conceptualization of what it means to be spiritual. It is about self-transformation through practice. This being the case, we can say that spirituality cannot be understood as knowledge (in the conceptual or objective sense in which we use the term), nor is it just about rationality or rationalizing. Second, it cannot be taught or learned, as we might presume with some other subjects, by gaining a mental comprehension of the process to be employed. You actually have to carry out the practices, techniques or strategies that relate to spirituality and reflect upon the effects. Third, spirituality and spiritual education are not just instrumental terms. By this I mean we cannot think of them as valuable just because we expect them to serve particular ends, such as making us more moral or less socially dysfunctional. These may be likely results but one cannot set out to 'develop someone else's spirituality' in order that it may serve these purposes. If you did so you would remove ownership of the process from the individual. Fourth, spirituality radically questions our whole notion of education if we think of education as telling young people what we already know, as though by being told this they in turn will come to know the same. In order to justify my claims it is necessary to investigate how any notion of 'spiritual' is embedded in meditation in some sense.

Meditation cannot be defined. The best we can do is say what it is not. In doing that we move towards it and understand better what the spiritual is not. As a way of doing this I have presented, below, sections of conversation with Krishnamurti for commentary and analysis. They are taken from 'Are You Not Saying What the Buddha Said?' a discussion with eminent Buddhist scholars and David Bohm, the physicist.[6] The passage I have presented is from an exchange with Walpole Rahula, an eminent Buddhist scholar and monk.

THE CONVERSATION: JIDDU KRISHNAMURTI AND WALPOLE RAHULA

Walpole Rahula: I have been following your teaching – if I may use that word – from my younger days. To someone who knows Buddha's teaching fairly well, your teaching is quite familiar ... What the Buddha taught 2,500 years ago you teach today in a new idiom ... Buddha says that when one is free from desire, attachment, from the self, one is free from suffering and conflict. And you said ... freedom is freedom from all attachment. That is exactly what Buddha taught ... very importantly, you always say that you must not depend on authority – anybody's authority, anybody's teaching. You must realize it yourself, see it for yourself ... Buddha said ... only accept it if you see for yourself that it is right ... This is exactly the Buddhist attitude – that you should not accept authority ... you must make the effort, the Buddhas only teach. There is no conflict between you and the Buddha. Of course you are not a Buddhist, as you say.

Krishnamurti: No, sir ... May I ask ... why you compare?

WR: This is because when I read your books as a Buddhist scholar ... I always see that it is the same thing.

K: ... does knowledge condition human beings – knowledge of scriptures ... of so-called sacred books, does that help mankind at all?

WR: Scriptures and all our knowledge condition Man ... knowledge is not absolutely necessary ...

K: ... I would like to question whether knowledge has the quality of liberating the mind?

WR: I don't think *knowledge* can liberate.

K: Does knowledge actually condition Man? Let's put it that way. The word 'knowledge' all of us surely take to mean accumulation of information, accumulation of experience, accumulation of various facts, theories and principles, the past and present, all that bundle we call knowledge. Does this, then, the past help? Because knowledge *is* the past.

WR: All that past, all that knowledge, disappears the moment you see the truth.

K: But can a mind that is burdened with knowledge see truth?

WR: Of course, if the mind is burdened, crowded and covered with knowledge ...

K: ... Most minds are filled and crippled with knowledge. I am using the word 'crippled' in the sense of weighed down. Can such a mind perceive what is truth? Or must it be free from knowledge?

WR: To see the truth the mind must be free from all knowledge.

K: Yes, so why should one accumulate knowledge and then abandon it, and then seek truth? You follow what I am saying? ... I am questioning in order to inquire.

COMMENTARY AND ANALYSIS

The following is, of course, my commentary and analysis. Having read it you may wish to construct your own.

The point of quoting these sections of discussion is to determine what exactly is the difference between 'knowledge', as we usually *conceive* of it, and what we might term spiritual awareness: that which Rahula refers to as 'the truth' and Krishnamurti as 'truth'. I am not taking Krishnamurti as being 'right' in his argument, rather I wish to inquire as to what emerges from the discussion if we take it seriously. The two participants are not perhaps, in any fundamental sense, in disagreement – yet there is a tension. I suggest this tension is precisely the one we find in education if we wish to take the spiritual seriously. Rahula wishes to compare teachings. Krishnamurti says, yes we can do that but to what purpose? Thus we find that Rahula's purpose and Krishnamurti's are different. For Rahula it is to be a scholarly discussion examining the Buddha's and Krishnamurti's teachings. For Krishnamurti that has no spiritual purpose. What matters is a different form of inquiry: questioning the nature and purpose of knowledge in order to determine whether it is of any spiritual benefit. Both parties actually agree on the answer – it is not. But for Rahula, tradition, that is knowing what the Buddha taught, matters in the sense of it being a vehicle, a support or a signpost to the truth (this is overtly discussed later in the conversation). In the Buddha's teachings we find it expressed in the parable of the raft and the idea of the teachings being the finger pointing at the moon (the truth).

The problem comes if we mistake the finger for the moon; the teachings for the realization of the truth, or as necessary learning before that spiritual aim can be approached. In a sense any disagreement over this is one of degree but Krishnamurti's point is that conditioning in the accumulation of knowledge actually militates against the capacity for spiritual awareness. Any form of knowledge, religious or scientific, will do this because of the effect it has on our notion of reality, on our mind. It will condition us to think of the world and our being in the world conceptually, dualistically, rationally, intellectually and encourage us to be concerned with ourselves, our progress, our identity as separate from others. We enter a conceptual captivity of which we know no contrary. But meditation is the contrary of this:

> 'The silence of the meditative mind is not within the borders of recognition, for this silence has no frontier. There is only silence – in which the space of division ceases.'[7]

Thus, Krishnamurti is saying nothing different to the Buddha or other eminent spiritual teachers, but he is pointing out what happens when you take the *idea* of meditation or the spiritual and encarcerate it in knowledge or tradition – you lose the plot. This is precisely what we have done in education. If we really want to take the spiritual seriously in education it is a matter of doing it, not talking about it or learning what others have said about it. This involves a radical change to what we call pedagogy. There is no learning about and learning from; there is no teaching, only inquiry; there is no knowledge, only reflection on practice. There is no instruction, only doing; no answers, only awareness. This means, of course, that your students are likely to raise important and critical questions about what we call education. These will not be new questions for them, it will just be the case that for the first time, in a serious sense, they will have the opportunity and permission to inquire into them within *their* 'education'. Out of this grow the seeds of spiritual awareness or, to put it differently, their recognition that their life does not have to be just the result of a particular social and educational conditioning.

DIRECT AWARENESS

Since the argument I have presented above depends on experiencing meditation I offer an example below which is particular to me in terms of the environment I live in. It can be adapted to your own. I have divided it into two stages but this is simply to give it a structure to follow.

Walking the beach

From distracted attention to focused awareness: I am walking the beach. I see the waves, the pebbles, the trees and the people. My attention moves to each of these in turn. At any point I am aware of just these different things. By focusing my attention, rather than let it be distracted into fleetingly noticing these things as they catch my ear or eye, I become more aware of them in turn. I can attend to a more detailed awareness and I become aware of them in a fresh, more particular way – almost as though I am seeing them properly for the first time.

As this happens so I stop doing two things. I stop naming 'this is a wave, a pebble, a person'. I just see. Also *I* stop seeing. There is just the seeing.

> *From focused awareness to holistic awareness:* turn from the seeing of one particular thing to the awareness of all that is there. Hear all sound together just happening; see all that is in your vision just happening. No things, just the process of change; no 'you', just change. No change, just as it is. Don't describe it to yourself, just be part of it.

CONCLUSION AND RETURN

Having read this chapter, return to the opening quotation and consider your own response to it. Does meditation as a basis for spiritual education confirm, deny or modify it? As a result of reconsidering it you may wish to make your own statement as a basis on which your own professional practice can be constructed, revised or confirmed.

NOTES

1 National Curriculum Council (1993) *Spiritual and Moral Development: A Discussion Paper.* York: NCC.
2 SCAA (1996) *Discussion Paper 6. Education for Adult Life: The Spiritual and Moral Development of Young People.* London: SCAA.
3 For an insightful discussion of this, see McCarthy, K. (2000) *Messier than the Models: Spirituality at the Chalkface.* Oxford: Farmington Institute for Christian Studies. See also Erricker, C. (1998) Spiritual confusion: a critique of current educational policy in England and Wales, *International Journal of Children's Spirituality* 3(1), 51–64.
4 This is now quite extensive. To gain an overview of it the *International Journal of Children's Spirituality*, Abingdon, Carfax, can act as a first resource.
5 In religious education we can identify this in *Model Syllabuses for Religious Education* (SCAA 1994), with their two attainment targets of 'learning about' and 'learning from'.
6 Krishnamurti, J. (1996) *Questioning Krishnamurti: J. Krishnamurti in Dialogue.* London: Thorsens, pp. 18–38.
7 Krishnamurti, J. (1973) *The Only Revolution.* Mary Lutyens (ed.), London: Gollancz, pp. 19–20.

Part 3:

Meditation in the Classroom

CHAPTER 12

Meditation as movement: reconnecting with the body

Gina Levete

BODY AWARENESS

Awareness of physical movement is one of the easiest ways to introduce students to the practice of mindfulness in daily life.

Mindfulness is to be like a bird perched high in a tree, surveying the surrounds from a vantage point. The state of mindfulness acts as a protector, there is less likelihood of doing or being harmed. For students, an effective way to cultivate this state is through reconnecting with the body. The suggested simple exercises are a first step towards mindfulness, they are a form of meditation.

Reconnecting with the body is like linking up with a forgotten friend. In the West most of us need to learn how to live less in our heads and more with our bodies. Conscious thought is at least ninety per cent focused on 'me' and 'having to do'. The mind separates itself from the body and thought patterns become negative, anxious and confused. The energy circulating through the body is then blocked, which causes further stress and tension. Yet the miracle is the body functions, breathes and repairs itself without conscious instruction from me.

The pressures and demands of daily life can build up and cause us to feel as if all the energy is up in the head rather than freely coursing through the body. These are the times when it helps to turn to the body and allow it to untie some of the knots. Bodies are miraculous instruments, microcosms of the universe through which life flows. The body gallantly carries on even when the thinking mind is in turmoil. It puts up with an amazing amount of abuse, from bad eating habits to overtaxing.

Reconnecting with the body means giving attention to posture, breathing patterns, inner rhythms, daily movements, energy and the language of the body. Living life as a thinking head rather than as the total body may mean ignoring the physical body's own sensitive system of communication. If the mind leapfrogs forwards and backwards in time anywhere but the present, little attention can be paid to the intelligence of the body. Unlike the mind, the body has no choice but to function and respond as part of the moment. Past and future can only be lived in the head. Only when the mind is present is it possible to listen to the body, and when this happens things seem to take care of themselves because the body is able to indicate its needs – the food it works best on, when it has had enough or too little, when it needs exercise or is being pushed too hard. The body is often more intuitive than the thinking mind. If it senses danger and its signals are ignored by the intellect, it relentlessly attracts attention until the warnings are registered. If we can learn to be aware that the total body – feet, ankles, legs, trunk, arms, elbows, hands, head, skin cells, brain, heart are as an intelligent a part of ourselves as any of the mental thinking going on, then this finely tuned instrument is able to act not only as protector, but an anchor which prompts a return to the present when the mind wanders about.

In one way we may be very aware of the body particularly in relation to its appearance and making the best of it, but this is not really body awareness, it is the mind projecting an image on to the body. An image which may involve a good deal of striving, dieting and exercising not for the sake of the body but for the sake of the image. How often do we jog, walk, run and exercise as a total body, so that there is only the running, the jogging, the walking? For most of the time this happens on automatic pilot because our easily distracted mind has separated itself from the action.

Reconnecting with the physical body is a crucial step towards mindfulness and learning to live in the moment. Not only this, it also instils a sense of personal control which helps prevent the mind going off at a tangent. Consequently it becomes easier to respond rather than react.

Living less in the head and more with the body is not a difficult thing to do. It is just a question of getting into the habit of connecting to the physical body from time to time throughout the day, being aware of both the body and its movements. Practice is the key to success. The following suggestions and exercises will help to establish this habit. They are offered as structures that can be adapted to meet the needs of a class of primary or secondary students, or indeed teachers.

EXERCISES TO RECONNECT WITH THE BODY

1. Standing posture
The basis for reconnecting with the body is posture, finding the right standing and sitting positions in which we can recollect ourselves so that the breath and energy can flow freely. There is no need to 'yank' the body into position, adjust it as little as possible. Instead let the mind send messages or visualizations, and soon the body will learn. Finding the right posture helps to open out the chest area and lengthen the spine.

Stand with the feet parallel about a fist's width apart. The weight of the body is between the legs and over the insteps, but feel the heels and outside rim of the feet also taking the weight. Feel the feet rooted in the ground, knees going forward and away. Connect with the energy in the lower abdomen. Visualize the chest opening out and the sternum, the little dip below the breast bone, lifting up and shining up and outwards. Widen the upper back and shoulders. Lengthen the spine. Let the neck relax and free the head. Imagine the crown of the head is holding up the sky. Ears are on a line with the shoulders. The chin will automatically tuck in. Your gaze should rest ahead at eye level as your chin is tucked in. Soften the facial muscles, soften the face. Cultivate a tiny smile so that it becomes part of your expression. The arms hang so that the energy can flow out through the finger tips. Let any tension or tiredness 'ooze' out. Visualize your skeletal form and feel there is a space and emptiness in the skull and bones. Feel an inner stillness. Listen to that stillness. Look around the room and observe the stillness of the objects in the room. Notice how they are placed. It is their placement that creates the stillness.

Feel still as a mountain. Visualize the mountain's stillness entering you. Feel the energy flowing through you like a river. Connect up with the three points, feet, head and lower abdomen. Close your eyes and be aware of the breath and your stillness. Shake out all over. Really shake as if you were a rag doll being shaken. Shake out like rain drops. Make sounds as you shake. Exercise the face by making ugly faces. Screw it up, stretch it out, puff out the cheeks, suck them in, twist it. The face becomes tense and set if it isn't given the chance to exercise as well.

Suggestions for daily practice: posture can be practised anywhere at any time, at the bus stop, in a queue. Rather than wait anxiously, turn your attention to your posture. After a time, by simply sending some of the suggested messages, the body will begin to adjust itself. If you are depressed, focus your attention on the sternum and visualize it lifting upwards and outwards. Continue to focus on this part of the body. You may even find yourself smiling.

2. Sitting posture

All the suggestions for the standing posture equally apply to the sitting position. For a right sitting posture the body needs to be held upright, as described for standing. Allow the spine to lengthen, slumping is out. Our usual tendency when tired or depressed is to sink down. This only worsens matters. The vertebrae of the spine are crushed together, blocking the flow of breath. The mind and the body become even less connected. Slumping can be a good feeling but from now on it has to be an occasional luxury.

Sit in a relaxed upright position, aware of the natural grace and dignity of the body. That means you. Shut your eyes and allow the face to soften. Allow all the parts of the body to soften and open out. Sit with the weight over the seat bones, the bony bit in each buttock. Let any tension or exhaustion drain away through the face, the shoulders, the back, through the arms, finger tips, legs and feet. Sit and be aware of the breath.

Suggestions for daily practice: when reading, writing, or just listening absorbing information, occasionally come down from the thinking head to notice the posture. Is it crouched, tense, twisted? Is the head poking forward, hands tense? If so, rest for a moment and gently allow the body to regain a comfortable posture. It will do wonders for the work in hand.

3. Breathing

For the most part, the body breathes itself without instructions from the conscious mind. However, mental tension will almost certainly cause physical tension, which in turn interferes with the natural flow of breath. This is when it is necessary to step in and consciously breathe deeply, until the normal breathing pattern resumes itself. The following exercise is for deep breathing.

Sit in an upright position. Turn attention to the lower abdomen, two inches below the belly button. With the mouth gently closed, inhale through the nostrils and slowly draw the breath down to this part of the body. The stomach will inflate like a balloon. Exhale the air from the lower abdomen up through the body, so that it is expelled through the nostrils. The stomach will now deflate. You could silently and slowly say 'filling' as you inhale and 'emptying' as you exhale. The exhalation should take longer than the inhalation. You will probably find there is a natural pause before inhaling again. If it is difficult to follow the breath, focus on the movement of the abdomen acting as a bellows filling up and emptying out.

Suggestions for daily practice: breathing in this way can be an anchor to focus on in states of anxiety or fear. For example turning your attention to the breath, inhaling deeply and exhaling slowly before starting an exam, or having an interview, can help to calm the mind. If you are angry and about to explode with indignation, or say things you may regret, come down from the thinking head. Turn your attention to the breath. Silently wish yourself peace as you breathe in, and as you breathe out.

4. One-pointed attention: a walking exercise
Walking is a very good way to reconnect with the body and the present moment. This exercise need not take up any extra time, it can be practised whenever it is necessary to walk from A to B, which could be up the corridor, to the bus stop, or during a proper walk.

Pay full attention to the action of walking. Feel the strength in your legs, notice how it feels as each foot connects with the ground, notice the pace of the walk. Feel the strength of your back, the head supported by the spinal column. Lift the upper part of your body off the hips to prevent digging the legs into the ground, because doing this places stress on the knees. Let the strength of the upper body carry you along. Return the attention back to the feet step by step as they connect with the ground. Rather than forcing the mind to focus, just enjoy allowing the body to lead and the feet and legs take you where you want to go. If only walking a very short distance, for example from one room to another, simply be aware of the feet as step by step they connect with the ground. On a proper walk, to help focus the mind's attention on the walking it helps to be conscious of the breath. At the start of the walk inhale deeply, as the walking continues exhale slowly in and out, in and out, aware of the feet as they connect with the ground. After a short while let the breath resume its natural rhythm and just enjoy the walk as a total body.

Suggestions for daily practice: if you are walking in surroundings which cause an uneasy feeling, instead of being affected by the situation and getting caught up by the chattering mind 'This is dreadful; why did I come?' bring your attention to the feet, the walking movement, the lengthening of your spine, the strength in your back as the crown of your head pushes up towards the sky. Don't look down. Your gaze should rest gently ahead of you at eye level. The walk is now your personal dance.

5. Ways to reconnect with the body during the day

During a school day remaining consciously in constant contact with the total body is unlikely to be possible. Even so, it is of real benefit occasionally to come down from the head to reconnect with the body if only for a few seconds. Learning to do this can be almost as good as taking a break.

Whether involved in physical or mental work, from time to time notice what the body is doing. Whether chatting with friends, working or doing the washing up be aware of the physicality of the task. During those moments place all the attention on the body. How does it feel to play or run? Whether using a word processor, writing, or listening to the teacher, for a few seconds come down from the head and reconnect with the physical picture. What is the language of the body saying: is it relaxed or tense? If listening, notice what the physical body is doing. Is it fidgeting, doodling with a pencil or still? Is typing getting the body down so that the back is slumped over the word processor? When with a group of friends is the body language aggressive, territorial or welcoming? Does the strain of an exam or interview tighten the facial muscles or show through the whites of the knuckles?

Reconnecting with the body means that the picture can be adjusted so that the body responds to the moment with composure.

6. The practice of one-pointed attention

Daily routine activities can be used as the subject for one-pointed attention, for example, the task of getting dressed or undressed. During the short time it takes to do this pay full attention to the physical movements involved.

Be aware of the action of pulling a sweater over the head, putting on a pair of tights, buttoning or unbuttoning a shirt, tying a shoe lace, eating, or drinking a cup of tea. Experience the physical feeling resulting from each action. Be aware of the muscles that are used for making a bed; the strength and movement of the back when cleaning the bath, or just sitting; the stance of the body when happy or depressed. How does the total body feel when climbing the stairs or reaching up to put something away? Pay attention only to the physicality of the activity and allow the thinking mind to take a back seat.

If it is relatively easy to pay full attention, extend the period of one-pointed attention to include another activity during the day. Practise each day with the same activity until the exercise becomes an established habit. When this happens even a mundane task like getting dressed can assume a quality, rather than be something so unimportant that it happens on automatic pilot while the mind is elsewhere.

Sometimes the thinking head pays a great deal of attention to what to dress the body in but this is not reconnecting with the body, it is the mind projecting an image. One-pointed attention, which allows the body to be the sole focus of attention, means the thinking mind has to have the courage to realize that at times it is dispensable and enjoy this fact.

7. Pauses: no exercise, no movement

An attractive approach already introduced in some schools is 'pauses'. This simple idea can have a positive effect, developing a sense of calm. It can also be an effective way of preparing very young students for meditation at a later time.

At the end of each teaching session/activity before students move to the next class/activity the teacher rings a small bell (not essential) which indicates a few seconds of complete physical stillness and silence. It is important not to instruct the student how to use the pause other than as a few moments of physical stillness and silence. Introducing pauses requires no alteration to a busy schedule. Its effect can be remarkable, instilling a sense of place on solid ground.

8. The body and sensory perception
To enjoy a heightened sense of sensory perception it is necessary to encourage students to let go of the baggage of the mind, at least for a time, so that there is a space to really see with the eyes, hear with the ears, to smell, taste and touch. Space to experience the wetness of water when washing the hands, to notice the small weeds pushing through cracks in a concrete pavement, or absorb through the body the colour of flowers, the magnificence of trees. Space to allow colour to reach out to the eye, rather than the mind reaching for colour. Mindfulness so that there is an awareness of the relationship between the tactile sensation of an object, and the hands that hold the object. Mindfulness of how the physical body rather than the mind feels when the weather is hot or cold, wet or windy.

Giving students the opportunity to explore sensory perception in this way, can bring them a sense of heightened awareness, which may permeate into other areas of their daily life.

9. Relaxing as a total body

Lie on the floor as a body. Let go of having to be or do anything. Let the floor support the weight of the body. Let all parts of the body rest and spread out. Let the brain rest, feel as if it is spreading out; let the facial muscles soften. Rest the back, the shoulders, the arms, wrists and hands. Rest the buttocks, the legs, the ankles, and feet. Let go of the body, let go of time, let go of now, just let go.

CHAPTER 13

Meditation and stilling activities

Michael Beesley

INTRODUCING STILLING

'I think the stilling has had a great effect on our class. After stilling we are more relaxed and ready to work.'

'Stilling is good because it lets me focus and think about things that I would never have time for.'

These comments, both written by boys, are typical of the reactions of members of their mixed ability tenth-year class when asked to evaluate the weekly 'stilling' exercises in their RE course. They illustrate how adolescents welcome opportunities to acquire and practise the skills of quiet reflection, and can recognize the benefits which flow from this kind of learning experience.

The wording of the 1988 Education Reform Act (ERA) legislation on Collective Worship in schools seems to contain wisdom when it requires worship to be a daily activity; for it seems to acknowledge that children and young people can gain much from having to stop their busy-ness at least once a day and give time to reflect on things which are of the greatest worth in human experience and understanding. It also seems to recognize that, to be effective, this kind of activity needs regular discipline and practice, in the same way that the skills of literacy and numeracy need regular practice to equip pupils for these aspects of learning and living. Stilling is a practice that can help equip pupils with these skills.

VALUING SILENCE

At the heart of stilling is the valuing of silence and quiet reflection. To develop an appreciation of the value of quiet reflection in any community, we need to acquire and practise four particular abilities:

(1) to enjoy the self-discipline of sharing quietness with others;
(2) to focus our thoughts so clearly that no one and nothing can distract us;
(3) to tune into and appreciate our sensory and imaginative awareness;
(4) to be open to the rich insights which may be discovered in meditative reflection.

Beginning

Most groups of young people respond positively when invited to try a new activity which they know others have found relaxing and enjoyable. A few basic rituals and ground rules are necessary to help a class to begin stilling with a sense of order and security. These might include:

(1) rearranging the furniture so that the group is sitting in a circle;
(2) invoking a change of atmosphere in the room by placing an attractive visual symbol in front of the pupils as a sign that the activity is about to begin, e.g. a lighted candle, a vase of flowers or an artefact which evokes tranquillity;
(3) telling members they will be invited to share their views about the activity when it is over;
(4) saying that groups enjoy and gain most from stilling when they do not distract each other;
(5) that the best way to begin is to let your body become still and quiet in a well-balanced way, with a straight back to maintain alertness.

It may also be helpful to say that no one can or should be obliged to take part in a stilling exercise if she/he does not wish to do so. However, anyone who does not wish to take part, should be asked to use the time for her/his own quiet reflection, and not do anything to distract others.

A listening exercise

Before any stilling exercise begins, pupils should be told what to expect; for example, they will be invited to concentrate on their listening skills and to notice for thirty seconds in turn what sounds they can identify outside the room, inside the room and then inside themselves. They should also be told that they are likely to be able to focus most clearly on sounds if they turn off their sense of sight. They can be invited to do this by closing their eyes or, if they don't like doing this, looking downwards at the floor so that no sights will distract them and they won't feel that others are looking at them. As the listening exercise is coming to an end, pupils can be asked to imagine for a few moments that they are making in their mind a list of the sounds they noticed. Then, very slowly and gently, they can allow movement back into their body once more, by moving their toes inside their shoes, stretching their shoulder muscles and arms, and, only when they feel ready, letting their sense of sight become open again to everyone and everything about them.

Debriefing

At the end of the exercise, pupils may be invited to talk quietly in pairs about the sounds they noticed and how they felt in the activity. Debriefing in pairs can empower everyone to speak and be heard, even the most shy. Then a full group debriefing can take place in which members are invited to say what they noticed and how they felt while doing the activity. After a stilling exercise, pupils often value an opportunity to express in writing or illustration what they discovered or how they felt during the exercise. An eighth-year girl wrote the following description of a basic breathing exercise:

Breathing – we sit with our feet on the ground and back straight. We sit still, then gently close our eyes. We feel the breath going out through our bodies. We feel refreshed with the clean air coming in and out, in and out.[1]

Progress and development

Each class moves at its own pace through the learning and practice of basic skills. A debriefing after each stilling helps a teacher to know the students' preferences, difficulties and when they are ready to be challenged by more demanding exercises. The debriefing gives students the opportunity to consider and take responsibility for difficulties and distractions and to discuss ways to overcome them. Most classes quickly come to value their regular opportunity to let go the pressures of the day, to relax and be refreshed by taking part in a basic sensory or breathing exercise, perhaps accompanied by serene music. Once they have mastered the basic techniques of stilling, class members may like to be invited to reflect in a more directed and demanding way on specific moral and spiritual issues, such as in a 'thought for the week', a theme from their study, or events within or outside school.[2]

GUIDED IMAGERY

'Until I did these exercises, I didn't know I had an imagination!' This remark was written by an eleventh-year girl after her first term's experience of stilling, after having changed schools. Pupils have much to gain from opportunities to explore within their imagination their inner sense of sight, sound, touch, smell and even taste, for example, on a visit to an imaginary beach.[3]

The beach

The teacher invites the group to become still, using a simple exercise to slow down their breathing, and then, with their physical sight turned off, to go in their imagination to a beach of their own choosing. At the beach, they can explore the nature of the beach with each of their senses, write their name in the sand or float on the shallow water of a safe and enclosed lagoon. A ninth-year girl described her experience of the beach in this way:

> My beach was empty and it had palm trees. It was an island beach and the sand was flat and yellow. The sea was clear blue and there was a dolphin swimming in it, chattering. When I walked down to the sea, the sand was warm and soft under my feet. I didn't have any shoes on so it was also going through my toes. When I sat down at the water, I had my knees up against my chest. When I drew my name in the sand, I watched each grain of sand that fell into the dip where each letter was. I was wearing a short red dress that flared out like the one in the ice-lolly advert. I was eating a strawberry ice lolly. My hair was a lot longer and it was all shiny and it was glistening.

USING STILLING ACROSS THE CURRICULUM

Stilling skills can support affective learning in many areas of the curriculum. For example, a science teacher enriches his students' understanding of photosynthesis by inviting them to use the stilling skills they practise regularly in their RE course. Having judged that the class has a good understanding of the basic processes of photosynthesis, he invites them to complement their cognitive learning by affectively imagining what it might be like to be very still like a plant and draw life-giving energy from the sun through their hands to every part of their body, as plants do through their leaves. This experience seems to enhance the students' understanding and attainment when they produce their account of this investigation for their science folder.

Example: guided imagery in history

A history teacher taught his class to find out about life in medieval times. Then he took them, by means of a guided imagery exercise, to a medieval market town. Each student had a particular piece of business to do, person to meet or articles to buy. With their eyes shut, they all experienced the journey to the town, the crowds, the animals, the smells, the nature of the buildings, the meeting places, the market stalls, and all the activity of the day. After the exercise, there were several moments of quiet recollection before an animated discussion took place in which the students wanted to share what they had experienced. The teacher used this 'guided imagery' exercise with one class, but not with another as a control group. Later, both classes were required to produce a piece of writing about life in medieval towns. There was no doubt in the teacher's mind that the quality of the work produced by students who had experienced the 'guided imagery' exercise was of a much higher quality than in the other class.

Reflecting on the death of Diana, Princess of Wales

When stilling is a regular part of students' school life, they may come to realize that they have skills which can help them come to terms with life's most thought-provoking situations. When an eleventh-year class, many with learning difficulties, arrived for their first RE lesson of the 1997 September term, it was apparent that they were deeply affected by the death of Princess Diana. Since 'stilling' was a natural and welcomed part of their life in school, it came as no surprise when they asked to share a time of silence reflecting on their thoughts and feelings about her death. They settled themselves with a breathing exercise and then spent 3–4 minutes in focused thought, with quiet background music. During the debriefing after the 'stilling', several members of the group asked if they could have time to express their thoughts in pictures or writing. An atmosphere of creative quietness followed. A range of outcomes was produced, which, despite their artistic and literary limitations, showed that most students had engaged profoundly with their reactions to Princess Diana's death. One student wrote:

> Remember, you'll always be the Queen of all our hearts.
> God bless you!
> I like the way I can now say she's at peace.
> I wish she could have been in peace when she was alive.
> With all the love you gave us,
> I just wish we gave you more back when you were alive.

GUIDED FANTASY

A guided fantasy exercise extends guided imagery by giving pupils an opportunity to explore in more depth aspects of their spiritual journey of response to life's most fundamental questions. These questions lie within every thoughtful person and relate to the way we try to understand, for example, our origins, humanity and individual identity, relationships, purpose in life and ultimate destination. Guided fantasies are most effective with classes who enjoy stilling and the companionship which can grow through sharing insights in the debriefing. A guided fantasy invites students to step into a story and become part of it. The story offers a scenario but does not prescribe the outcome, nor the particular insights which may be discovered within it. 'The River' is one such exercise.[4] It invites participants to imagine they are on a long journey. They come to a wide river, with no means of crossing. A stranger rows a boat to the bank of the river and offers to take them across. During the crossing, they can talk with the stranger about anything they wish or just remain in silence together. As they say their 'goodbyes' at the other bank of the river, the stranger gives them a folded piece of paper to be opened on the next stage of the journey. A ninth-year student wrote very fully about this fantasy, including these comments about the rower and the message:

> I knew it was God. His loving eyes and caring face brought a warm sensation to me. I felt I could trust him with everything I knew and felt. We sat there for a while in complete silence. I said quietly, 'What will the rest of my life be like, do you know?' God looked at me and smiled but said nothing ... When I was far away, I sat down and opened the piece of paper; it read, 'Your life will be happy because you are loved and you love many people.' I felt tears come to my eyes, and remembered the beautiful, loving, caring face of God. He had answered my question.

CONCLUSION

When class members build a sense of ownership of their stilling time, individuals readily acknowledge the value of acquiring skills and techniques for achieving calmer lives in stressful situations and for enjoying imaginative reflection on the wonder and mystery of life. Nearly all will undoubtedly appreciate, like Tia, their regular opportunity to let go of the pressures of the day and be refreshed by a time of relaxation and focused reflection. She wrote, 'I always feel fresh or happy after meditating; for the rest of the day I don't usually argue or get uptight over things.' Many will enjoy discovering and expressing experience within their imagination, like Daniel who said, 'When I'm in this exercise [the beach] I am near a lagoon and I am safe and warm. It's good because [the exercises] let me focus and think about things I would never have time for.'

Some will unlock within themselves a spiritual awareness which enriches their attitude to life and gives inspiration to others. The following poem came from a Christmas holiday homework assignment in which eighth-year students were encouraged on Christmas Eve to stand under the night sky and, after a few moments of reflection, to write down a list of key words to express their thoughts and feelings. They were then asked to shape these words into a poem. Charlotte produced this response:

The glittered stars	The sky is deep
Are like eyes	It's never ending
Watching over us	Going on forever
Keeping us warm	Until nothing
The silent sky	The sky holds beauty
So quiet, so safe	And it holds memories
Holds mystery	Of seeing the Saviour
And secrets	Being born.

NOTES

1 Scripts for exercises of this nature can be found in: Beesley, M. (1990) *Stilling: A Pathway for Spiritual Learning in the National Curriculum.* Salisbury: Salisbury Diocesan Board of Education; Nash, W. (1992) *People Need Stillness.* London: Darton, Longman & Todd; Stone, M. (1995) *Don't Just Do Something, Sit There.* Norwich: Religious and Moral Education Press; Murdock, M. (1987) *Spinning Inward.* Boston: Shambhala.

2 Beesley, M. (1992) in Diaries of Reflection, *Space for the Spirit.* Salisbury: Salisbury Diocesan Board of Education.

3 See the publications listed above for further examples of guided imagery activities.

4 Scott, A. (ed.) (1989) *Insight.* Taunton, Somerset: Somerset County Council.

CHAPTER 14

Meditative techniques from the Buddhist tradition

Clive Erricker

AWARENESS

There is a Zen story about a professor of great repute visiting a Zen master, Nan-in. He came to him to learn about Zen. Nan-in poured a cup of tea, but when his visitor's cup was full he kept on pouring. The professor watched this until he could bear it no longer. He implored, 'It is overfull, no more will go in.'

Nan-in replied, 'Like this cup you are full of your own opinions and speculations. How can I show you Zen unless you first empty your cup?'[1]

This story is indicative of the most salient message that religious traditions offer on the subject of meditation: stop thinking and start observing. Observation, in this sense, is like just listening. There is no need to react, form opinions or judgements but just to be aware. This awareness can be understood in two ways: awareness of what we observe outside ourselves and awareness of what we observe within. The latter is concerned with our thoughts and emotions. These are not intrinsically different but we tend to categorize them differently because we rationally divide our experience into the world outside us, and we, the 'I' who is in the world. With regard to meditation we can adjust our understanding through the following exercises. The object is to just be aware, in the moment, of what we observe and see it as it is; don't react as though you must make a judgement on it.

The first activity focuses on observing a tree. Trees are not special in this respect; after all, Anando, the Buddha's disciple, became enlightened by the Buddha holding up a flower. The teacher's skill lies in offering the right experience at the appropriate time. You may wish to choose a different object.

Activity 1. Observing the tree

Trees are both ubiquitous and symbolize free growth – they don't need tending; and yet we take them for granted. To observe their presence and character without our intervention has a powerful effect. They may be the majestic result of hundreds of years of history or just small saplings, it is of little consequence.

Sitting in front of the tree observe its detail: the bark, the trunk, the branches, its leaves. Observe and absorb each aspect in turn. Then consider its growth, from a seed through its roots to what you see before you. Let your students dwell upon the change that is taking place slowly and inexorably before them. A tree is not a thing but a living organism. We can touch the tree and feel its texture in its changing parts: roots, bark, leaves. What do we receive from that experience? The importance of the experience is that we do not think about trees and what we think about trees; we just observe them and return with our reflections on that experience. This we may turn into poems, drawings and discussion but most significantly we return with meditative observations that do not concern the use or value of trees in relation to our own purposes. In other words, we have observed dispassionately, not according to our own perceived needs, desires or opinions.

SPACE AND SILENCE

We are used to identifying what is positively there as opposed to the context or framework in which it happens. So, for example, we notice noise without recognizing the silence within which noise occurs. This recognition of the context or presence of silence or absence is another way in which mediation in religious traditions has sought to influence our perception. We can regard it as something positive, not negative. Lao Tzu, as the reputed author of the Tao Te Ching, put it in the following way by saying:

'The Way is like an empty vessel
That yet may be drawn from
Without ever needing to be filled.'[2]

This we can relate to the quality of silence in the following activity.

Activity 2. Listening for the silence

Listen closely to the noises you can hear. As you listen focus on those that are softest or least obvious. Include the noises you are making with your breathing or as you shift your posture. Then, beyond these, focus on the silence that exists between the noises that attract attention. Stay with the silence between the noises and return to that as the noises occur. What happens when you stay with and return to the silence?

METTA: LOVING KINDNESS

The meditation activities above have an impersonal quality, but religions are also concerned with the generation of particular virtues. In the Buddhist tradition one of the principal meditations for this is called Metta Bhavana, generating loving kindness. This activity focuses on developing that quality.

Activity 3. Meditation on loving kindness

Metta meditation begins with the usual prescriptions to comfort the body and attend to the breathing found elsewhere in this book. After relaxing the body, by following its contours with the mind and mentally letting any tension flow out of it, we start by silently repeating 'May I be well' as we breath in and 'May others be well' as we breath out. To focus this bring to mind a friend or relative whom you are fond of. As you repeat the phrases see them with closed eyes in front of you and extend your goodwill to them. Feel their response as you sense their presence. See them as clearly as you can and feel their good wishes coming from them towards you and entering your chest. Stay with that feeling and image for a short while before ending the meditation.

To extend the meditation further we think of others in need of our thoughts. Those within the class we are in and those beyond: friends, relatives, those whose company we enjoy and those we don't. Also others we know are in need. 'May we be well, may all beings be well.' Hold these images in mind until the meditation ends. Before finishing come back to yourself 'May I be well.' Give yourself back the energy to give out after your meditation.[3]

INNER SPACE

We are used to the idea of observing what is outside us, in the world, and the idea that, by behaving appropriately, we can and should have some beneficial effect. We are less used to dwelling on how that beneficial effect can come about. We do not give in a negative state of mind, rather we attack – we arrange our relationships around our own feelings. This can frequently have negative effects which we have to repair later when we are in a better frame of mind. The following meditation is offered as an antidote to the haphazard way in which we often construct our relationships. It is a meditation on anger and its destructive effects. Again, following the usual procedures for calming the mind, introduce this activity.

Activity 4. Meditating on anger
In the Buddhist scriptures we find the following teaching:

> Suppose an enemy has hurt you
> In what is now his domain,
> Why try yourself as well to hurt
> Your mind? That is not his domain.
>
> If you get angry, then maybe
> You make him suffer, maybe not;
> Though with the hurt that anger brings
> You certainly are punished now.[4]

The point is that anger is a powerful energy that takes hold of us and prevents us from responding appropriately. It does us harm because it causes us to hurt. Seeing anger for what it is and letting it subside by not holding on to it is a healing and empowering activity.

As a meditation bring to mind something that still makes you get angry. It may be something that somebody repeatedly does which annoys you. With my family it is no one clearing up dirty crockery or washing it up. It may be something that happened today that you haven't quite let go of and forgotten yet. You may want to start with a class by discussing these things before doing the meditation.

Sitting still just let the feeling of your anger be there in your mind. Be with that feeling - just watch as though you are at a distance from it waiting to see what it does. Do not try to hold on to it, i.e. don't *think about it*, just watch it. Do this for a minute or two and see what happens. At the end you can discuss this. Don't discuss the anger, but what happened when you tried just watching it. It can be useful, after this meditation, to follow with the one on loving kindness.

INSIGHT

Buddhists talk of two types of meditation: *samatha*, which calms the mind, and *vipassana*, which means insight, watching the mind. As an extention of the meditation on anger we can go on to watching the mind.

Activity 5. Watching the mind

With this activity it is good to start by representing the mind as something, creating an image or embodying it. In Zen it is likened to a bull. The idea is to tame the bull. Normally we think of taming as gaining control over something by forcing our will on it. But here the point is to stop the mind, our thoughts and emotions, gaining control over us. I like to think of the mind as like a squirrel, because we have a young squirrel in our garden. As I watch it eating and burying nuts its busyness and acrobatics can be seen as like the mind's constant activity. Also, like the squirrel, the mind is harmless in itself, only when we become trapped in the views and opinions, feelings and emotions that pass through us is damage done.

In the Jain scriptures we find another analogy, that of two birds: eating bird and watching bird. Eating bird is what we think of as our mind, constantly active and concentrating on doing things. We can also be watching bird, watching the busy activity of the mind going on without being trapped in it. In this way the mind is recognized for what it really is, we discover its true nature. We are not it and it is not us. It is fun to ask students to find their own animal to represent the mind. It is also more purposeful because they gain ownership of the activity from the beginning.

First let the mind become calm by relaxing the body and focusing on the breath, then watch what arises and what passes away. Do not attempt to think things into the mind, but watch what thoughts pass through. Don't try to stop and analyse them; just be aware of their presence in what would otherwise be an empty space. Don't try to empty the space either. The point is not to try and do anything. Notice when a physical sensation comes into the mind: an ache, discomfort, hunger; when a feeling or emotion arises: happiness, sadness, boredom; when a desire or memory appears creating wishes, longing or embarrassment. Notice the intention and reaction that form in the mind in response to these things. Pay attention to the process of thinking rather than the content of the thoughts. 'Allow thoughts to be like waves on the surface of a vast ocean, or like clouds floating in an incomprehensibly vast sky of mind.'[5] It is good to end this meditation by coming back to the breath, the body or silence as the focus of attention.

After this meditation it is good to discuss what happened. Some students can feel frustrated at getting caught up in their thoughts and not noticing this happening. Others can be genuinely unaware of what happened or confused as to what they were trying to do. These issues are bound to arise when doing something that contradicts our usual behaviour and expectations. They should be seen as positive outcomes as part of a learning experience that is new. We are so used to seeking to achieve things and be successful that it comes as something of a shock to be affirmed for noticing what was 'not achieved' or identifying 'what went wrong'. Like when we first attempt to ride a bike or swim, what matters is to have a go at something that at first may seem impossible and want to go back and do it again.

Here is some final advice from St Francis de Sales:

> If the heart wanders or is distracted, bring it back to the point quite gently ... if you did nothing ... but bring your heart back, though it went away every time you brought it back, [you] would be very well employed.[6]

NOTES

1   This story and many others can be found in Paul Reps (1971) *Zen Flesh, Zen Bones.* Harmondsworth: Penguin Books. Such stories in Zen parlance are known as 'Mondos', with the purpose of aiding enlightenment or awareness.

2   Tao Te Ching, ch. IV, repr. in Eliade, M. (1997) *From Primitives to Zen.* London: Fount, p. 595.

3   A valuable commentary on this can be found in Ajahn Anando (1989) Kindness and Insight, in *Seeing the Way: Buddhist Reflections on the Spiritual Life. An Anthology of Teachings by English-Speaking Disciples of Ajahn Chah.* Hemel Hempstead: Amaravati Publications, pp. 78–89.

4   *Visuddhimagga*, 308.

5   Levey, J. (1987) *The Fine Arts of Relaxation, Concentration and Meditation: Ancient Skills for Modern Minds.* London: Wisdom Publications, p. 112.

6   Ibid., p. 65. St Francis here uses the term heart, but the terms heart and mind are interchangeable ones in meditation. They are two different words between them covering the notion of consciousness. Although St Francis is a Christian, he speaks a language understood across different religious traditions.

CHAPTER 15

Meditation and story
Clive Erricker

THE IMPORTANCE OF STORY AND NARRATIVE

'Almost too readily we believe that, in our electronic age, the habit of storytelling has been lost so that we have stopped expecting it to operate.'[1] Stories are what we create to remind us of ourselves and our world. They are the way in which we make sense of our experiences. The habit of storytelling never ceases but we can become unaware of it. A good teacher needs to be a good storyteller, but importantly children and young people need to be able to affirm their own stories about themselves and become good listeners to the stories of others. I regard this process of telling and listening to stories or narratives as fundamental to education. When we introduce stories, our own or from literature, they need to be instrumental to the purpose of empowering the listener rather than just the teller. If this happens, the story will connect with the experience of the listener and the listener will turn into a teller, he or she will own the story his or herself. Ownership will mean reflecting on the meaning of the story within one's own experience. Introducing meditation into this process deepens the reflection and focuses it, leading to a new awareness. It also makes us consciously aware of the storytelling process we usually employ only unconsciously; in other words it makes us self-aware of how we create our 'selves'. This realization empowers us to take control of, and responsibility for, our own stories or narratives.[2] The following three examples indicate different ways of engaging with this process.

1. THE PATIENT BUFFALO

The story of the patient buffalo comes from the Jataka Tales.[3] These are a collection which recount the former lives of the Buddha before his birth in human form. Each one is about a particular animal who embodies a specific virtuous quality or qualities. Patience or restraint is a much underrated quality because we can tend to see it negatively. The Dalai Lama put it this way:

> People think patience is weakness. But I think not. Anger comes from fear, and fear from weakness. So, if you have strength then you have more courage. This is where patience comes from.[4]

However, knowing what patience is and developing and using patience does not come from talking about it. You must come to know it by experiencing it. That is what we are going to use the story of the patient buffalo for.

> A water buffalo is grazing in an open field, chomping at the grass with big teeth and lips. This buffalo is particularly big and strong. Above him, on the branch of a tree, sits a mischievous monkey intent on some fun. He decides to taunt the buffalo. First he jumps down onto the buffalo's back and dances around on it. The buffalo carries on chomping. So the monkey thinks 'How can I get this buffalo annoyed?' He decides to swing on the buffalo's huge horns. But this has no effect either. Finally this particularly mean monkey thinks he must get the buffalo to react if he treads down the grass in front of him, so that he is unable to grasp it with his mouth. The monkey is disappointed yet again as the buffalo takes no notice. At this the monkey decides the buffalo is no fun and he will go elsewhere to annoy someone else.

Not to be overlooked in the story is the point that the buffalo could have been tempted to use his strength to get rid of the monkey. He could have done something about it but chose not to.

The story comes alive if performed as a simple drama, rather like a pantomime, involving the audience telling the buffalo what to do, with you, the teacher, encouraging them with questions. This also helps the children to own the story themselves and creates the important ingredients of humour and fun. This will also bring about the contrast in atmosphere with the meditative activity that follows.

Meditation activity

> Turning to the meditation, now sitting still, explain that we are being like the buffalo, waiting for the monkey. The monkey will only come if we are perfectly still and wait. In preparation we can listen to see if we can hear him. Start with listening to the loudest sounds, then a quieter sound, and then a quieter one still. Explain that you know when the monkey is there because you get an itch. Wait for the itch but don't scratch it. Just let it be, watch the itch, keep your attention on it. After a while the itch goes away. Then it comes back somewhere else. You know the monkey is still around, but don't scratch the itch. Sometimes the monkey does not give you an itch but does other things to distract you. Sometimes he makes you feel hungry, or makes you feel sleepy or gets you to think of other things. Do thoughts pop up in your mind? Watch them. Do they go away again? Just watch and see what the monkey does when he gets into your mind.

This idea of the monkey in the mind can helpfully focus attention in the meditation and be used afterwards in recognizing that thoughts and feelings can distract us if we let them. In relation to patience we can gain some confidence that we have the resources to restrain ourselves in situations rather than just react, and recognize how things can turn out differently if we do that. This allows us to discriminate and make reflective judgements rather than impulsive ones. We can also admit when we have acted in a heedless way because we know that we can act otherwise. This makes for valuable conversations about ourselves and our actions rather than just trying to obey injunctions like 'be patient' without the strategies to do so. When children move on from the activity into other work or out from the class tell them to watch for the monkey. You know he is there when you become irritated by something. Rather than react, just watch the irritation. Let it calm down or go away before you do anything. Then tell the story of what happened and what you learnt from that.

2. KRISHNA AND RADHA

In the Hindu tradition Krishna is one of the main and most popular Gods. Loving devotion to God, Bhakti, involves a different type of meditation. Behind this is the notion of Darshan – seeing, or being seen by God. The idea is that being seen by God, coming within his or her sight, one is blessed. Through devotion then one receives the qualities God bestows as one is drawn closer to him or her. Thus one becomes more saintly by drawing on God's presence in one's own heart. In the mandir (temple) and in puja (worship), before a shrine, this is the intention. We can borrow from and adapt this understanding so that it can be used outside a religious and strictly devotional frame of reference. With that intention in mind we can use a story about Radha and Krishna and incorporate another strategy that is again borrowed from the Bhakti tradition. In repeating the name or names of God, saying mantra, the devotee is again drawn closer to him. To aid this malas are used. These are beads on a string, similar to the Catholic rosary. As the mantras are said so the beads pass through the hand. The Hare Krishna mantra is an example of this, 'Hare Krishna, Hare Krishna, Krishna Krishna, Hare Hare.' We begin with the story.

> The story of Radha and Krishna tells of how they grew up together in an Indian village. When he was young Krishna looked after the cows and Radha was one of the milkmaids or gopis. Krishna had a great sense of humour and liked to play tricks. One example of this was when he found the gopis playing in the river. Their saris were lying on the river bank. Krishna took the saris and, climbing a tree, hung them on the branches. Then he said in order to get them back the girls would have to give him a kiss. This they all duly did until it came to Radha. If he wanted a kiss, she said, he must come into the water to get it. So Krishna took off his own clothes and entered the river. When he came close enough Radha pushed him under the water and swam to the bank. Her clothes were still up the tree so she put on his. People looked at her strangely when she walked back to the village, but they laughed loudly when Krishna walked back in hers.

So Radha was smart and Krishna didn't always get his own way. But as they grew older and wiser their affection for each other grew into love. Krishna, on his journey through life, eventually becomes the God who is worshipped now. Radha represents the human soul which finds its home in devotion to Krishna. This bliss or love is captured in our story when Krishna and Radha are alone together for just three days on an enchanted island. After that Radha must leave to return to the realms of hell where she struck a bargain with Yama, the lord of the dead, that she would return if she were allowed to see Krishna just once more. Why she is there is another story, but hell is simply the place without love or belonging. As Yama said 'There is no home in hell. All here are exiles.'[5] And exile is the absence of love that we all sometimes have to endure. Eventually the story ends happily with the dance of the rasmandala, the great unbroken circle within which all souls are united with God or, to put it another way, find Love.

Meditation activity

Telling the story leads on to the meditation. In a circle, our own rasmandala, we close our eyes and look into our hearts. Who do we find there who makes our own heart dance? See that person clearly. They are smiling at you. You smile back. Feel the energy they give to you. What quality is it that they give to you: is it kindness, generosity? Can you name it or is it better just to feel its presence? Stay in touch with it for a short while, perhaps a minute or two. As you come out of the meditation bring that quality with you to pass on to someone else.

After the meditation stay in the circle. Give a bead to each person or ask each person to come and take a bead to give to the person next to them. Pass round the string to go through each bead in turn. Make sure there is a knot in the end to stop the beads falling off. When the string comes back tie both ends together. You may do this so that the beads are on a large circle of string or so that the beads are close together. If the former, each person has in their hand their own bead, representing the quality and person they experienced, in front of them. As they turn it they silently bring the name or quality back to mind. If the latter, you can now pass the class mala around, moving to each person in turn. As they receive it they turn the next bead and then silently say the name or quality as a way of bringing it back to mind. If possible, all this should be done in silence, apart from any practical instruction you give.

3. THE TEMPLE BELLS

This story is an adaptation of one with the same name written by Anthony de Mello.[6] When telling the story it is good to alter the mood as you go through, moving between humour and lightheartedness, to silence and seriousness. I point out at the end some strategies for doing this but you may find your own. It is better if the story is interactive. Again, there are some notes at the end on this.

The type of meditation used here moves us towards the idea of a journey as found in guided imagery. It is also more akin to the way in which Krishnamurti used the term. In his journal he describes scenes at particular places where he had stayed and given retreats. In the main these were reconstructed from memory. Thus he used the recollection of a place and the sense of being there as a meditation, or as a way of encouraging awareness, and forgetfulness of oneself. Here is one example to set the scene for the story that follows and the way it is used.

> Coming over the stile into the grove one felt immediately a great sense of peace and stillness. Not a thing was moving. It seemed sacrilegious to walk through it, to tread the ground; it was profane to talk, even to breathe ... to enter this grove not knowing what lay there was a surprise, and a shock, the shock of an unexpected benediction ... Come when you will and it will be there, full, rich and unnameable.[7]

The story of the temple bells
When he was young a boy used to have a story read to him in bed about a temple and, because it was his favourite story, his parents read it to him again and again. The story told of a temple in a far-off land that had a thousand bells. When these bells rang they made the most beautiful sound in all the world, and people came from all over the world to hear them. As the boy grew older this story stayed with him. But, in the story, there was a moment when the temple was destroyed by a huge wave and the ruins were carried to the bottom of the sea. Yet, so it was said, it was still possible to hear the bells if you sat on the shore and listened patiently and silently enough. When he grew up the boy set out to go and hear these bells. He travelled a long distance to the island, where he sat quietly on the beach to hear this most beautiful of sounds. For a whole year he sat there every day, but all he heard was the sound of the gulls in the air, the wind in the trees and the waves on the shore. After a year he decided to go home, disappointed. But before he did he went to the beach to sit for one last time and listen to those sounds with which he had become so familiar and which he had come to love: the gulls, the wind and the waves. As he did so, sitting silently and still, he waited until he heard the most beautiful sound he had ever heard.

Meditation activity

After telling the story ask the listeners to do the following:

(1) close your eyes and go back through the story in your mind;
(2) choose your favourite moment;
(3) put your hands out palms up next to one another;
(4) transfer your favourite moment from your mind into your hands and close them together;
(5) turn to the person next to you and tell them what you have in your hands and why;
(6) discuss your conversations with the whole class, if you wish, and explain why you think you chose the moment you did.

When telling the story, introduce moments at which everyone stops and listens and sees images in the story with closed eyes; in other words, use the story, in part, as a form of meditative activity. The purpose of the ritual and sharing, at the end, is to transfer the story to the listeners and encourage them to link it with their own experiences and reflections. This can then lead into further expressive and creative activities. However, before doing anything else we remind ourselves that we still have the moments from the story in our hands. We have to make a decision as to what we are going to do with these. It can be a group decision or individuals can decide differently.

At the end of the story and activity that follows it I distribute a shell to each of the listeners and say that they can now tell the story to someone else by using the shell. Thus the story can start from the object that has now become a symbol or image by virtue of it embodying the story and that individual's reflections on it.

Sometimes I do not tell the ending, but ask the listeners to imagine their own ending. Did he hear the bells? Or, what did he hear? (i.e. what did you hear?). Over time and with many tellings the story has come to incorporate embellishments; for example, a café/inn where the boy stayed when he first arrived on the island, people in the café whom the boy asked if they had ever heard the bells, etc. This has involved the listeners role-playing these people. Responses then become incorporated in the next telling of the story, and so on. The important thing is, of course, not the particular story, nor the specific activities, but the process employed, and adapting the content and the telling to the age of the group and their responses.

NOTES

1 Meek, M., Warlow, A. and Barton, G. (eds.) *The Cool Web: The Pattern of Children's Reading*. London: Bodley Head, p. 7.
2 Two excellent examples of this can be found in Marsha Hunt (ed.) (1999) *The Junk Yard: Voices from an Irish Prison*. Edinburgh: Mainstream Publishing. Also, Dorothy Allison (1996) *Two or Three Things I Know for Sure*. New York: Plume.
3 There are many versions of the Jataka Tales in English for children. I have found the following useful: Khan Noor Inayat (1985) *Twenty Jataka Tales*. London: East-West Publications. The Patient Buffalo is on pp. 87–90.
4 The Dalai Lama (1996) *Kindness, Clarity and Insight*. New York: Snow Lion, p. 39.
5 These words come from a telling of the story in N. Frith (1976) *The Legend of Krishna*. London: Abacus, p. 150. This is my preferred source for the story but it is now out of print. All my children were brought up on this as a book at bedtime with a chapter per night! There are other sources but the main thing is to tell it in your own style with due attention being paid to the reverence for Krishna as a God, and Radha as his consort, in the Hindu tradition. To aid the telling you may wish to use pictures of Krishna and Radha or Krishna and the gopis dancing the rasmandala. These are available, often through organizations like Tradecraft, ISKON (International Society for Krishna Consciousness), or Tantric Designs, as are malas.
6 In A. de Mello (1984) *The Song of the Bird*. New York: Image Doubleday, pp. 22–3.
7 Krishnamurti, J. (1982) Brockwood Park, Hampshire: September 14, 1973, *Krishnamurti's Journal*. New York: HarperSanFrancisco, p. 9.

CHAPTER 16

Meditation and science: developing a contemplative frame of mind

Jane Erricker

The combination of science and meditation in a title might seem like an unusual one. The reputation of science as positivist and rational does not sit easily with an understanding of meditation as intuitive and contemplative. However this is a misunderstanding of science. The best science, the original and innovative science, has always involved contemplation and intuition, as Kuhn identified when he described revolutionary science. The majority of scientists, those wedded to the traditional scientific method of verification, work within such a tight framework that they are unlikely to see anything outside it. If one is to leave oneself open to new ideas and insights then one has to develop a frame of mind that gives a space for new thoughts to enter. This involves a stepping back from the minutiae of manipulating variables, establishing controls and verifying hypotheses and allowing oneself to see a bigger picture. Particularly, one has to see where one's observations do not fit, and instead of ignoring them because they do not contribute to the verification, consider what they might mean. Scientists who make ground-breaking discoveries are those who see this bigger picture by stepping back from the problem. They observe closely and mindfully and, by contemplation, allow their minds to make original connections.

When teaching science in school there is a danger that we will be so focused on teaching the skills of investigation that we forget that the skills of mindfulness and contemplation need to be developed as well, if we are to encourage at least some of our pupils to become real scientists. This is partly because the process skills of investigation are hard to teach even without complicating the issue with more elusive skills, and partly because the time available for teaching science, particularly at primary level, is becoming more and more limited as the curriculum becomes more crowded. However, the skills that I am suggesting be taught and developed are generic skills, and they are useful elsewhere in the curriculum: other chapters in this book have identified where this might be. They are also part of spiritual and moral education, and now part of the new subject of citizenship, so we can justify the time and effort spent in activities such as the ones I will describe here.

These activities are basic science activities, as they would be taught in the primary classroom. However they are easily adapted for older children and anyway they are intended to be just an indication of how you can move seamlessly from cognitive learning to a meditative activity and back again. I'm sure that teachers can find many more science opportunities to practise these skills. What I shall describe here are specific meditative opportunities that might be used in the everyday teaching of science in order to enhance science learning. More detailed descriptions of the contemplative exercises referred to can be found elsewhere in this book.

POND DIPPING

Pond dipping involves the collection of samples of water, including their resident small animals and plants, from ponds or streams or lakes, or even from rock pools by the seashore. The intention is to see the variety of living organisms that live together in a single habitat, to identify them, and to consider the relationships that exist between them. Samples can be collected using sophisticated apparatus that enables the accurate collection from the surface, part way down in the water and from the bottom of the pond, or the collection can be more casual, using a net and a bucket. The collecting vessel must always contain water from the host pond, and the children must be aware that the creatures collected must be treated with respect while they are examined in the classroom and returned to their original habitat reasonably quickly. Science texts can give detailed instructions on how to collect from a pond so I will not describe it in detail here. I am more interested in what happens when the samples are examined in the classroom. When the samples are brought in a small amount of water with its residents can be put in a white plastic tray so that it can be examined. At this point the children can often see nothing. They stare into the water and see nothing because they don't know what they are looking for. What is needed here is a moment of relaxation and of centring, so that the children can concentrate and allow themselves to see.

> Instead of striving to see, with the mind rushing about aimlessly, just observe in a focused and detached way. See into the water, watch and wait. Just be aware of what is there. Move your attention carefully and slowly. Patiently notice what you can see. Concentrate only on watching and waiting for things to appear to you.

When the children have achieved the right frame of mind they should be able to appreciate the hundreds of tiny organisms moving about in the water and the huge variety of structure and methods of locomotion and nutrition. If the children use magnification to examine the creatures in more detail there is more opportunity to consider with awe and wonder the ingenuity of the natural world. It is my experience that children overcome the initial, sometimes learned, repugnance for 'creepy-crawlies' if they are given contemplative time to really see how fascinating and complex they are.

CANDLES

In primary science, candles are used in the topic of change. We light candles and ask the children to observe them very carefully and describe what they see. Again, close observation is facilitated by a moment's centring and contemplation.

> Just see the candle. Observe its whole shape ... Focus on what is happening in detail ... Follow the process of the candle burning.

We expect the children to notice the different zones of colour in the flame, to see the melting wax forming a liquid pool at the top of the candle and then running down the sides, only to become solid again, to notice the grey smoke escaping from the flame, which increases in density when the candle is blown out. The wick and the candle itself are consumed as they are allowed to burn for some time, and the children can do a planned investigation by weighing the candle before and after burning, and they can consider where the wax and wick have gone. Why is there very little debris left? Where has the candle disappeared to?

The explanation is scientific of course because there are chemical changes, for example burning, going on here, and physical changes such as melting, evaporating and solidifying. All of these can be discussed and explained. But then, as well as using meditative skills to enhance the process skill of observation, candles themselves have much richer associations with religious and meditative practice that can be identified and reflected upon during what was initially a science activity. There is no reason why these different aspects of the curriculum, and of skills development, cannot be combined. The symbolic nature of the flame in many different religious traditions can be discussed and the associated stories can be told or read. Aspects of the scientific nature of the flame, for example its ephemeral nature, can be connected and used to explain, in part, its use as a symbol. Its symbolic nature can, in turn, be used as a matter for reflection.

EARTH AND SPACE

The topic of earth and space is traditionally used as one that can encourage a child's imagination and can allow a child to grapple with difficult abstract concepts. The topic involves appreciating the huge distances in space, the very large sizes of planets and stars, and aeons of time. Although the descriptions and explanations are scientific, there are gaps that can only be filled by leaps of the imagination. We use models and computer programs to illustrate the positions and sizes of the planets and stars, but the child's imagination has to superimpose these on the real world because he or she cannot get in amongst them. As before, in other topics, concentrated observation and contemplation helps the child to see the night sky, and, with older children, it is useful for them to try to imagine the huge distances involved, even infinity. This is best done as a meditative exercise. One useful method of checking that children have understood some of the aspects of the topic is to take them through a guided fantasy.

The children are asked to close their eyes and to imagine that they are rising up from the ground inside their classroom. The teacher asks them questions about what they feel like and what they can see.

Imagine that you are rising up from your seat and that you have reached the ceiling. Look down on your classroom. What can you see? (the tops of the tables, the heads of the other children).

Now imagine that you have passed through the ceiling and outside the school. What can you see now when you look down? (the roof of the school, the playground, the road outside the school, people walking along the pavements). What can you see when you look up? (the sky, the clouds, night or day sky, the sun, the moon).

Imagine you are moving up into the sky and looking down on your town. What will it look like? (like a map, you will see the roofs of the buildings, rivers, the sea, boats on the sea).

Imagine you are above the clouds. What do they look like? (like cotton wool). What might they feel like? (they are water vapour so they will feel wet, like mist or fog). What would you see if you looked up? (the blue sky).

Continue your imaginary flight up into space. Look back at the Earth. What does it look like? (like a ball, you can see the blue seas and the green and brown land and the white clouds drifting above them). Why are some lands green and some brown? Look up into space, what does it look like? (black, with stars).

Keep going into space. Which planet do you reach next? What might it look like?

You can continue this imaginary flight for as long as the children can sustain it. You can ask questions that focus on aspects that you have covered in your lessons and assess the children's understanding of the structure and positions of the planets, comets, meteors, etc. With older children you can ask what happens after you have passed the known universe, and discuss their ideas later.

OURSELVES

In the topic of Ourselves the children learn about their bodies and how they function. They do investigations into their senses including the functioning of their eyes, ears, sense of smell, of taste and of touch. They learn about their internal organs and the processes of breathing, digestion, excretion and transport within the body. They also learn about their muscles and energy conversion in the body. Meditative techniques can be very useful in developing the children's awareness of their bodies, and, in conjunction with scientific knowledge of their bodies' functioning, can foster a healthy lifestyle.

The children can be invited to sit quietly, close their eyes and relax their muscles. Naming each part of their bodies and asking them to first contract and then relax each part can help them realize that they have muscles in their feet, legs, stomachs, etc. and can, for younger children, simply help them to learn the names of each body part. When they are relaxed they can be encouraged to become aware of their breathing, breathing slowly and mindfully. (Small children must be reminded not to hold their breath for too long.) When they follow each breath in their imagination, down into their lungs, they can be aware of each structure that the breath passes through. This exercise can be developed into a guided fantasy similar to the one described for Earth and space, but a journey within the body rather than outside it. The air can be followed into the nose, with hairs and mucus for cleaning and warming the air and receptors for detecting chemicals (smell). Then the air passes down the back of the throat into the trachea, where the vocal cords are, into the bronchi, bronchioles and finally the alveoli, where gaseous exchange takes place. The changed air can then be followed back, making a sound as it passes the vocal cords. The movements of the muscles of the rib cage and the diaphragm can be followed as breathing takes place.

Although the breathing exercise has a more obvious connection with meditative practice, you can undertake this kind of internal fantasy journey through any structure of the body, for example the blood system, or the digestive system. The explanations and descriptions given by the children allow the teacher to judge their understanding of the topic.

Another more classic meditative exercise, walking meditation, also encourages body awareness.

Note the sequence of movements as you walk. Standing, lifting, moving, and placing one foot and shifting your weight. Then lifting, moving, placing and shifting your weight to the other foot. Begin by moving slowly. Move no faster than you are able to move with complete awareness. This is not a moving meditation so much as an exercise in developing a continuity of mindful awareness. At times experiment with moving more swiftly, simply noting each time a foot touches the ground. Be loose and natural. Experience the flow of movement, moment to moment, with awareness.[1]

The children can be encouraged to be aware of each muscle group as they walk and the shift of weight can be related to the forces involved (gravity, body weight). Joel Levey's book (see Note 1) contains many other exercises that can be connected to science topics by adding scientific knowledge to the instructions and to the subsequent discussions of how the children felt when they were doing the exercises.

In conclusion, the kinds of techniques and exercises suggested here may be found challenging by someone wedded to the idea of science as completely rational. However, our scientific understanding of our world is still very limited, leaving plenty of room for contemplation and the imagination. In addition our understanding of how people learn is also limited, and I would suggest that the techniques employed above positively enhance the learning process. It is interesting to speculate about the efficacy of the old-fashioned and discredited methods of learning, such as chanting mathematical tables, which may have worked by bypassing more rational thinking and opening up the mind to learning. I would be interested to hear about your experiences of using any of the above techniques and how you and your children enjoyed them.

NOTES

1   Levey, Joel (1987) *The Fine Arts of Relaxation, Concentration and Meditation: Ancient Skills for Modern Minds*. London: Wisdom Publications, p. 119.

CHAPTER 17

Meditation, creative expression and music

Leo Nolan

MEDITATION, CREATION AND CELEBRATION

The relationship between meditation and creative expression is not obvious, even to many meditators, as I have found in researching this chapter. The relationship has, however, been explained with typically unaffected depth and simplicity by the great twentieth-century teacher Sri Ramana Maharshi when he stated:

As you awake, the world awakes for you[1]

One of the most recent scientific disciplines, cognitive psychology, appears to confirm an insight made some twenty-five centuries ago in the Indian Upanishads (Hindu scriptures) and early Buddhist scriptures. The Chandogya Upanishad puts it like this:

that which (within the heart) is smaller than a grain of rice or a grain of millet, smaller than the kernel of a grain of millet, is yet, greater than the earth, greater than the heavens.[2]

In meditation, we not only find our place within Creation but, more mysteriously, Creation finds its place within us. (Every child knows that you only need to cup your hand over your ear, to hear the sea inside you.) Through meditation we are, as it were, wired up to the main power supply, and we come out of meditation awakened to ourselves as co-authors of, and characters in, the dynamic and ever-renewing Story of Creation.

In 1929, with World War I still a vivid memory, C. H. Dodd, the Christian teacher, made this remarkable prophecy:

If we could all become artists over the whole of life, using our whole environment to express the highest spiritual relations within our reach, is it not possible that the influence of humanity upon the world might change its whole aspect?[3]

These words were largely ignored; we allowed madmen to do our dreaming for us, and in little more than a decade after they were written, the world was plunged into World War II.

To realize and rediscover our role as artists is a responsibility. Fortunately, it is a joyous and loving responsibility. I am not talking about writing symphonies or painting triptychs, but rather of bringing our whole being into play, in preparing a meal, decorating a room, telling our children a bedtime story, teaching other people's children how to read. The fully alive, fully awake teacher becomes, in this context, not so much a distiller of external information, but rather, an amplifier for the inner voice of the higher self.

My own work in schools takes place within a wider community context and invariably ends with a celebration: a concert in an old people's home, a lantern procession, a small part of a large-scale summer carnival. Celebration is the sport of Shiva (the third god of the Hindu trinity), the dance of life, and forms the final link in the perpetual circuit of:

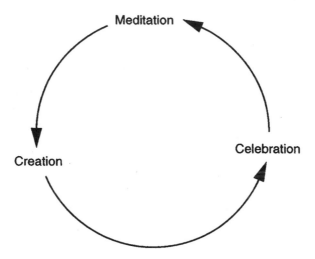

These are three aspects of one reality. In meditating, we simply are. In creating, we become actively aware of our constantly created and creative selves. In celebrating, we enjoy our being together. The totality of meditation, creation and celebration involves a movement from isolation to wholeness, from alienation to integration. A possible series of workshops would go something like this:

A. Listening
Music forms a natural bridge between the world of ideas, words and images, and the meditational sphere of pure consciousness. I often introduce meditation by gently striking a chime bar and asking the children how many notes they hear: 1, 2, 3, 4, 6, 10, 12? A few more strikings, requiring close attention and deep listening, reveal more and more sounds to the ears of the children. Any meditational technique involving concentration on a single point, can be said, by analogy, to sound a harmonic which fills the whole being, just as the chime bar fills the room. It is worth pointing out that there are some sounds we cannot hear at all, although our pets can.

For older students, with even a passing interest in sound recording, a more sophisticated analogy can be taken from the basic physics of sound. The science of psycho-acoustics poses the fascinating riddle that there exist frequencies which affect the brain and consequently the whole body but which cannot be recognized by the ear. Similarly, the sounding of the mantra (a word or short phrase repeated continuously during meditation) works in such a deep but real and physical way. (Music students are interested to learn that composers such as Chopin and Debussy made particular use of harmonics in their compositions for piano.) Referring back to the need for deep, wakeful listening, I would then teach the basic upright posture and give an explanation of the particular meditational method in use. I can explain the practice of meditation which I use like this:

---

1. Sit still, with your back straight.
2. Repeat a mantra (a word or short phrase) silently and continuously throughout the time of your meditation. The mantra could come from sacred scripture if you belong to a faith tradition. For example, a Hindu may use the phrase 'Hare Krishna' (meaning, 'Hail to Krishna'); a Christian, 'Maranatha' (meaning, 'Come Lord'). A word like 'love' or 'peace' might be appropriate, or simply the repetition of your own or a friend's name. The point is, not to concentrate on the meaning of the word, but to listen interiorly to the sound of it. Generally, I play a guitar gently for a minute or two then allow the appropriate length of silence. (The length of the meditation depends upon the age of the child. A rough guide is to allow a minute for each year of the child's life. For an adult, twenty minutes is considered a minimum, thirty minutes an optimum.) I would then play the guitar again to indicate that the children should gently cease to say their mantra and, when they are ready, to open their eyes.

B. Composing

I would then give the children their first commission – to compose a piece of music for meditation. This needs to be two minutes long and they must be able to repeat it exactly, in order to tape the piece twice, once as an introduction to meditation and once more at the end of the meditation. This exercise has been pitched at all ages and ability levels, from lower juniors to professional orchestras. It also adapts itself to whole class or group work. A discussion concerning dynamics, tempo and appropriate instrumentation obviously constitutes the first step in the proceedings.

To tighten the structure, I would suggest the construction of a graphic score based on a theme. It can be abstract, realistic, or a mixture of the two. A whiteboard, blackboard or a roll of paper can be used with chalk or felt markers. Most schools are now familiar with graphic scoring (the use of visual images or symbols, rather than traditional musical notation). Some discussion may be needed to reinforce the collective requirement that symbols need to be mutually agreed upon, before or after the creation of the score. The process can then be constructed as follows:

1. A volunteer may be asked to draw a symbol which he or she considers autumnal.
2. Several more volunteers could be brought forward to complete a score, which may look like this:

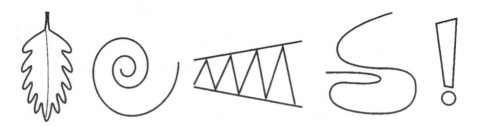

3. A volunteer conductor would then follow the score with her baton and agreed sounds be made on violins, chimes, dustbin lids, or whatever is to hand. The structure could be tightened further by suggesting that the children make only one sound, at only one point on the score:

e.g.

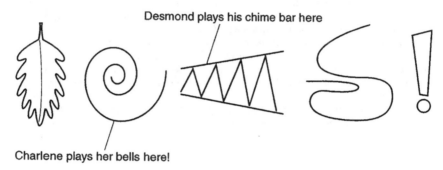

Desmond plays his chime bar here

Charlene plays her bells here!

The children need to listen and concentrate carefully and deeply, in order to create and re-create a collective score such as this. They need to make responsible choices in terms of their relationship with other instrumentalists. Do I play at the same time as Jo or a bit later? Should I play a bit softer on my cymbal so that Collette can be heard on her recorder? And so on.

A slightly more sophisticated development is to create songs out of the most ubiquitous and least-used items of school equipment, the metallophones or wooden xylophones. My own approach is to take most of the bars off the instrument, leaving a pentatonic (five note) scale. C, D, E, G, A is one of the most common, but any existing five-note scale or a made-up one will work. The children cannot go out of tune and almost any combination of notes will sound fine. The stages of the activity are as follows:

1. Take the children out for a walk in the playground or a nearby park, if there is one. Help them 'see' what there is around them. Help them look closely at the colours and patterns in nature and have them describe what they see and feel. Make ample use of metaphor and simile.
2. Back in the classroom, either in groups or with the whole class, have the children remember their experience and elicit from them their words and phrases. A year-five group in one primary school during autumn, produced: 'The autumn moon looks like a spinning jenny floating to the ground like a leaf'. Through the editing process, this became:

The Autumn Moon falls like a leaf
Spins like spinning jennies.

3. I then had one child repeat the phrases as expressively as she could, and then followed her intonation as closely as possible, in the form of a diagram on the blackboard:

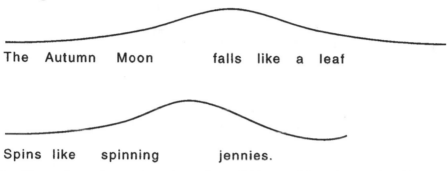

4. Notes from the pentatonic scale could be positioned onto the diagram like this:

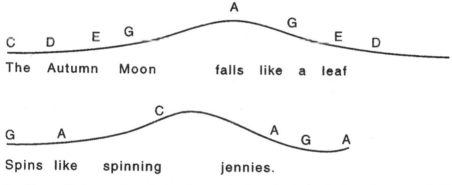

5. I would have the class clap out the rhythm of the phrase and if appropriate, given the experience and ability of the children, notate the rhythm in a separate diagram like this:

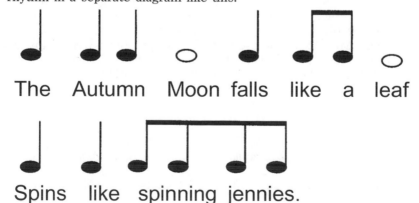

6.   From this, again, where appropriate, a simple score can be developed by effectively merging the last two diagrams like this:

By adding each group's contribution, a unique, composite piece, without necessary repetition, would emerge. This type of composition would be classed as 'Through composed'. Monastic plain chant is an example of such a style.

C. Celebrating

This is a simple example of collective creativity which could develop into a celebration. This could take place in the classroom or outside in the playground or in the school garden if there is one. A most effective development would be to take the children out of the school altogether into their immediate community. A beautiful example of this type of celebration is the lantern procession, an utterly magical and increasingly popular community activity. For example, in High Bentham, near Lancaster, for the past few years, children from the local County Primary School, under the direction of the extraordinary Celebratory Arts Company, Pioneer Projects Ltd., have been processing around their village with their home-made lanterns (see fig. 2.) and giving out their home-made pots of jam to older residents. As they stop at each door they perform their little piece of music and sing a short thank-you song. The particular glory of the lantern procession is that it is, paradoxically, secular and sacred at the same time. It uses elemental imagery: light and darkness, delicacy and strength, sharp contrasts of scale. Flickering candles in their willow-and-tissue lanterns reflect the moon and stars within the vast depths of night, while transient humanity crawls ant-like upon the ancient, self-restoring Earth.

  To end where we began, these children are at the beginning of what could develop into a lifelong process of becoming artists over the whole of life, using their whole environment to express the highest spiritual relations within their reach, to paraphrase C. H. Dodd's prophecy. If such an example were to become a more integral part of our children's education, is it not possible that the influence of humanity upon the world might indeed change its entire aspect?[4]

NOTES

1   Ramana Maharshi *Ulladu Narpadu*, p. 36, 3–4, 10, 37–40, in A. Abhishiktananda (1974) *Saccidannanda: A Christian Approach to Advaitic Experience*. Delhi: S. P. C. K.
2   From the *Chandogya Upanishad*, p. 12, 3, 14, 2, in A. Abhishiktananda (1974) *Saccidannanda*.

3   Dodd, C. H. (1978) *The Meaning of Paul for Today*. London: Fount, p. 33. Dodd is here referring to St Paul's concept of the spiritual transfiguration of the material world, made visible in the person of Jesus Christ and in the active life of Christians.
4   As for the creative activity described in this chapter, most of it comes out of practice developed over several years and owes almost nothing to textbooks. I would always advise teachers to work with experienced and inspirational artists rather than from books. The most important teachers for me over the years have been: (1) for music, Peter Moser, More Music in Morecambe, The Hothouse, 13–17 Devonshire Road, Morecambe, LA3 1QS; and (2) for celebratory arts generally, Alison Jones, Pioneer Projects Ltd., 32–34 Main Street, High Bentham, Lancaster, LA2 7HN. The best source for schools looking for musicians working in the community is the Community Music Organization: Sound Sense, Riverside House, Rattlesden, Bury St Edmunds, IP30 OSF, tel. 01449 736287, fax, 01449 737649, e: *100256.30@compuserve*. Your local Arts Board will also be helpful.

CHAPTER 18

Meditation and Special Needs
Leo Nolan

INTELLIGENCE AND WISDOM

In our time, there is a particular status and reverence given to intellectual achievement. The insidious consequence of this is a tendency to give low status to those who appear deficient intellectually. As a result, much 'Special Needs education' stumbles along with sub-standard equipment and inadequate overall facilities. A Nissan hut containing a broken cymbal and a couple of drums with their skins missing remains all too often the reality behind the rhetoric.

Interestingly, when Paul of Tarsus was writing, the cultural milieu was remarkably similar. Comparing his own teaching with that of his contemporaries, he remarked:

> We teach the things that no eye has seen and no ear has heard, things beyond the mind of man.[1]

He concludes this train of thought with the following radical conclusion:

> Make no mistake about it. If any one of you thinks of himself as wise in the ordinary sense of the word, then he must learn to be a fool before he can really be wise.[2]

In meditation, we are gently led beyond the contingent realities of thoughts, images and words towards 'the things which no eye has seen and no ear has heard!' Here we are all on a level playing field and it would be unwise to come to Special Needs education with the condescension of a supposedly superior intelligence.

MEDITATION AND COMMUNITY

When people meditate together they become a community; strangers become friends. All traditions of meditation carry the belief that meditation is an energetic, rather than inert, activity. Moreover, the underlying assumption is that this energy is open, trusting, compassionate, loving. The community created during meditation becomes, consequently, a community of compassion, a community of love. Meditators, as well as practising daily by themselves, frequently come together in community, usually once a week. This period together is an important source of strength, of mutual support.

The Special Needs class, even the one in the Nissan hut with the leaking roof, becomes a secure environment, where we can explore our individual and collective potential, by means of communal meditation (whilst still militating for the roof to be fixed). In such an environment, it naturally follows that no one is put down, ridiculed, categorized, made to feel 'bad' or 'wrong'. Of course this approach is important in every branch of teaching but in Special Needs education, it is critical. Even now, and the situation is changing, people with learning difficulties spend so much time being told to be quiet, to regulate their behaviour to societal norms, in order not to stand out or draw attention to themselves. Meditation is a liberating experience, opening the door to the infinite potential within each person.

SPECIAL NEEDS, SPECIAL GIFTS

The term 'Special Needs', whilst being preferable to earlier pejorative descriptions, has the danger of sectioning off or marginalizing a diverse group of people as if they were a tribe. The truth is that, just as everyone has equal access to wisdom, everyone equally possesses special gifts and special needs. Let me give an example. On one community music project, I assembled a group of musicians which included members of Manchester Hallé Orchestra, a band of Irish traditional musicians and dancers, and a Special Needs group from a local Day Centre. The Hallé musicians, whilst being able to play beautifully from a written score, had problems improvising and composing. I would describe this as a Special Need. The Special Needs group, however, could compose and improvise, having practised such skills during sessions with a community musician.

As an example of special gifts: one of the highlights of this project occurred during one of the workshops, when two musicians embarked upon an improvised xylophone duet. The absorption of the two was total, first one then the other taking the lead, changing melody, tempo and dynamics, according to an intricate, instinctive musical system of sublime creativity. The absorption of the audience was equally total and the whole effect genuinely transcendental. It should come as no surprise by now to learn that one of the musicians is a nationally recognized percussionist, the other a man categorized as having Down's Syndrome. In that room, at that time, these two individuals were demonstrably equals. Experiences like this are rare, precious and special but, at the same time, equally accessible. An Indian saying states:

An artist isn't a special kind of person, but each person is a special kind of artist.[3]

To find this artist inside ourselves is, to my mind, one of the central aims of learning. The practice of the art of meditation is one way of accessing this invaluable search to the creative centre of our being.

MEDITATION IN PRACTICE

Despite being constantly told that meditation won't 'work' with this or that particular group, although I occasionally come across individuals who choose not to meditate, I have yet to meet a group who, as a whole, as a community, do not 'take' to meditation. This certainly includes people with severe learning difficulties, even those who cannot keep still for more than a few seconds in any other circumstances (to the amazement of many a carer).

This book is full of a variety of meditational techniques, all equally valid and useful with Special Needs groups, albeit with the necessary adaptations. My way of teaching works like this:

The first task is to establish the physical side of the process: we first of all need to sit in such a way as to keep the back as upright as possible, using a suitable chair or cushion. (Finding a suitable chair can be quite a task, especially if people have physical disabilities. I have used cushions, blankets, stools and the like to ensure a straight back and a comfortable firm base for the feet.)

A mantra meditation

I then introduce the idea of a mantra. Mantra is a word from Sanskrit (the language of Indian scriptures) which has now, of course, passed into common speech. In its original context a mantra is a word or phrase repeated continuously throughout meditation. I often introduce the mantra by having the individuals repeat the name of a good friend or relative, or even their own name. Repeat it over and over with your eyes gently closed, until we forget the person whose name we have been repeating, and just listen to the sound for its own sake. Now, breathing naturally, slowly repeat the mantra in your mind or heart, from the beginning to the end of your meditation. If your mind wanders, and you realize that you have stopped saying your mantra, gently go back to saying it.

The duration of the meditation is important. Generally speaking, the period would last for five to ten minutes for people with moderate learning difficulties and two to five minutes for people with severe learning difficulties.

Timing and setting

The setting out of the room where meditation takes place is important, and should be done before people enter. It should be clean and tidy, and most meditating communities sit in a circle to reinforce their sense of unity. I have placed a candle in the room and sometimes fresh flowers, but while beautiful, simple, universal symbols like these add to the atmosphere, they are not essential. I invariably play a tape or CD of gentle music, or strum a guitar as people enter the room quietly and take up their positions gently.

Music

The choice of music to soothe people into meditation needs careful attention. Style is less important than content, which should be gentle and relaxing – for example, the sound of Japanese flutes, or sounds from an Amazonian rain forest. An effective method is to tape a two-minute section of music, leave a two- to twenty-minute gap, and record the first music again, to bring people out of meditation.

The ideal scenario is to lay aside a period in the day, at the beginning, middle or end, where the whole community, Day Centre, College and so on, have at least the opportunity to meditate together. Planting meditation into the daily routine makes it less eccentric, less of an accessory. Meditating is, after all, as natural as breathing. In my own practice as a music teacher I generally begin the sessions with a meditation. In the first moments after meditation, I tend to use exercises which reinforce that vital and natural marriage of the Self and the Other.

Finding our voice

We may stand up from our chairs, slightly bend our knees to straighten the spine, relax the shoulders, rolling them backwards and forwards, giving our full attention to the part of the body we are attempting to relax. Then we breathe deeply from the diaphragm. This exercise can be carried out with a partner.

In pairs, one stands behind the other and places their hands gently upon the other's ribcage. If the breathing is deep enough, we can feel our friend's ribcage blowing up like a balloon. This supportive physical contact is helpful. To creatively visualize the diaphragm as a rubber bowl plunging up and turning itself inside out with each deep breath can help.

Breathing in through the mouth, rather than the nostrils, makes it easier to draw in much more air. Again, in pairs, we can ensure that our neck is straight and relaxed.

For the first couple of breaths we can breathe in and breathe out silently.

For the next breath we breathe in silently but on breathing out we produce a small sound, so small that only the person producing the sound can hear it.

On the next outbreath, we produce a sound that our immediate neighbour can hear.

On the next outbreath, we produce a sound that the person opposite can hear.

On the next outbreath, we produce a sound that the wall or window opposite can hear.

Our final sound should be such that we are able to break the window opposite or place a crack in the wall, but don't scream. Ask someone to volunteer, after this, in producing a firm but gentle sound. The rest of the group can try to copy it or produce a harmony (the definition of harmony here being *any* note produced which is different to that of the volunteer).

After this warm-up, we might start singing popular music we are all familiar with, or perhaps new songs from Africa or Asia, and then, crucially, singing songs we have written ourselves. This strong sense of self (the true one, as opposed to the false one – 'Big Ego'), the trust and confidence engendered by genuine communion with others, which is the core of meditational practice, is actualized, made concrete in the community, a community which is then able to go out into the world, confidently, compassionately and joyfully.

As meditation reintegrates an individual personality, reuniting body, mind and spirit, the whole body or community becomes whole. And here, once more, we in the West are indebted to the contribution of Paul of Tarsus to social philosophy and to our understanding and appreciation of corporation and co-operation. Paul made a direct link between spirituality and practical social organization which is being re-evaluated in our time. The theory goes something like this: If there is one spirit, which animates, gives life to the individual, there is also one body which takes its shape and personality from its members, individuals who are bound by one law, one rule, one social norm only: 'the obligation of love, for love is the fulfilment of the law'.[4]

THE INDIVIDUAL WITHIN THE GROUP

We need to be clear that meditation is not an end in itself. The aim is not to be 'good' at meditating. It isn't another skill to be acquired like Maths or English. On the contrary, meditation is about not acquiring, not wanting. It is the way of dispossession, of unlearning, rather than learning. Meditation may observably lead to calmer classrooms and clearer minds, but these are by-products. The core of meditation is all to do with selflessness. For this reason, meditation, even when inserted into the curriculum, needs to have its difference respected. It needs to be set slightly apart. It has, in other words, its own special needs.

This may seem highly theoretical, but it has very practical applications for children who are seen, or see themselves, as being apart, as not quite belonging in the classroom or in the statistics. In the average modern classroom, where students with learning difficulties are integrated, a period of silence, even a very short one, at the beginning, middle (before lunch) and at the end of the day can be a wonderful sign of unity. To be different is not to be separate. Individuality gives character to the whole. In my own experience, even teachers who are initially suspicious of meditation see this sort of practice as offering 'added value' to the school day.

Silence has, furthermore, been used imaginatively in conflict resolution in some schools. At the Galloway Small School, where children of all abilities study together:

> vexing problems sometimes lead to silence as everyone thinks out solutions. It is so powerful and increasingly rare in kids' lives. That still small voice![5]

This is not strictly meditation as it involves thinking, but at least silence is brought to bear on a complex issue. I have myself meditated with children who have been in conflict with each other. I have also meditated with individuals who seem at odds with themselves, unable to settle into an integrated environment, especially if they have come from a school entirely devoted to children with learning difficulties. These efforts have proved helpful within the context of a caring school environment.

Meditation isn't an anaesthetic. It is about being fully awake, not half asleep, nor is it a panacea. Meditation is a long haul, involving a twice-daily discipline. When my teacher was asked the classic unanswerable question, 'How long will it take?' by a frustrated inexperienced meditator, the teacher replied, 'Oh, not very long. About twenty, twenty-five years or so!' Meditation may or may not be essential to the growth of the human spirit. There are obviously shining examples of selfless, integrated, compassionate and confident individuals who do not meditate. However, for a growing number of people, their twice-daily meditation has become the pivotal point of their lives. While self-analysis within meditation is counter-productive, the observation of the transforming effect of meditation in the lives of others is immensely rewarding. Like yeast, meditation does not alter the composition of the dough. It can, however, make it rise.

NOTES

1 1 Corinthians 2.9.
2 1 Corinthians 3.18.
3 Ananda Coomaraswamy.
4 Romans 13.8–10.
5 Letter from Vivien Jones, Head of Care, Galloway School, Carronbridge, near Thornhill.

CHAPTER 19

Introducing meditation to young people with behavioural and emotional difficulties

Jacqui Dye

INTRODUCTION

I have been working as an educational Special Needs teacher in a large junior school in North Bristol over the past ten years. In that time I have witnessed many changes in the way in which the curriculum has developed and how it is delivered to pupils. This has had a huge bearing on the provision of education regarding those pupils with educational Special Needs. It has been during this time of upheaval that I decided to rethink the way in which I, as their support teacher, worked with such youngsters.

The past ten years have also been perceived as a time of social change which has resulted in schools having to not only teach differently, but also deal with increasing numbers of disenchanted youngsters. These children bring challenging behaviour into our schools and playgrounds. They respond to the pressures forced upon them through tantrums, aggression, withdrawal and depression. There is less and less time to acknowledge, let alone address, the problems children bring into the classroom.

From my experience, I would argue that effective education and learning cannot take place if pupils are dysfunctioning. It is right that we should be teaching our children to read and write and to be numerate in school. There is also a necessary emphasis placed on the acquisition of scientific and technical knowledge which provides invaluable skills for the modern world. There is an attempt to cover a huge range of other subjects, to provide a broad-based curriculum, but in order to deliver education and for a child to receive it the whole child must be taken into account. With league tables and testing, the pressure is on for results but the playing field is not level and a large number of schools have to deal with social problems and inadequate funding which hold them back in the race for excellence.

Schools under pressure from such funding and the public's demand for high standards has resulted in the increase in suspension and exclusion of pupils. There are times when this is the only course of action, but reductions in budgets for more appropriate, creative and imaginative approaches in dealing with such behaviour have lessened the possibility of these numbers being reduced. I believe that we are creating long-term problems from short-term solutions. I would suggest from my own experience that there is at least one alternative approach which works and that is the introduction of meditation into children's everyday lives, working hand in hand with their learning.

I intend to write about my experiences using meditation with youngsters, many of whom had behavioural difficulties in addition to learning difficulties. As a result their behaviour was often unacceptable and challenging to both other children and to staff. Having been interested, throughout my career, in how children learn and why some do not, I had used different strategies to address the needs of the pupils with whom I worked. I was fortunate in being allocated my own room in which to work. This was unusual in that many support teachers work in corridors, corners of classrooms or any other available space. When I initially set up the room I wanted it to be a stimulating environment in which children would enjoy learning. It was filled with bright and varied posters and learning aids as would be seen in any primary classroom. I was able to accommodate a wide range of support which had a beneficial effect on pupils' learning and behaviour.

When priorities in spending changed as a result of government directives, Special Needs support of this kind became a luxury which could not be afforded. Cut-backs meant that staffing and support were drastically reduced and rethought. Added to less support, schools were being asked to take on heavier workloads with greater accountability. Children with behavioural difficulties were finding class work more frustrating as, in order to get through their day; a high degree of concentration, co-operation and application was required.

GETTING STARTED

I needed to think how best to use the limited time I had working with groups and individuals. This time had to be of value and used efficiently with careful planning. My day involved working with diverse groups of children from throughout the junior school. Timetabling had to be carefully thought out and I wanted the children themselves to be responsible for remembering their sessions.

Children who find it difficult to manage their behaviour find change and disruption hard to deal with. I wanted to build their sense of respect towards others in the school, when waiting for their sessions and when leaving and returning to their classes. It had also become apparent to me that, whilst coming to their sessions for support they often had issues, anxieties or stories they either needed or wanted to share. With the pressure to get down to work in class often these were not being heard. This was not due to unsympathetic staff, but to sheer time constraints and workloads. Indeed, staff would often ask me to talk to pupils who were causing concern and we were able to work together to sort out many difficulties.

At the end of another hectic and exhausting summer term, I decided to change the way I had been working. I had become increasingly interested in the holistic approach to teaching children, one which was concerned with the whole child and his or her well-being, acknowledging whatever a child brings into the classroom; feelings, strengths and weaknesses, and how these affect their learning.

I thought out a colour scheme for the room of pastel shades. I and the wonderful support staff working with me, went ahead and repainted it. We hung muslin curtains over the windows to soften the light and to shut out the distraction of the school drive. I asked parents to make us cushions for our meditation sessions, for which I cleared a space away from the main part of the classroom. I removed bright distracting posters and replaced them with others in pastel shades. I brought in natural objects such as stones and plants and burned lavender oil before the children came in. I also used tapes of natural sounds to set the atmosphere in which we were to work together.

Another way of working

I started with the very first groups which came to me in the autumn term. I was confident that the new pupils, who had moved up from the infant school, would accept that we worked in a different way together but I was anxious about the reaction of older pupils who had worked with me in the past. It was a new year so I was ready to try something new.

I intended to work with these youngsters so that I could immediately start addressing some of the concerns I had about them and the way in which they viewed themselves and others. I intended to connect with the positive goodness I believe is in us all. I wanted the children to begin feeling better about themselves and to start recognizing that they could become more focused on the tasks they would be working on in their sessions with me.

Why meditation?

Through practising meditation myself I knew first hand the benefits it provided. For a short time before the busy day began, I regularly took time to centre myself and stop the rush of thoughts through my head, to find a place of stillness and peace inside me. As a result I found I could work more effectively. It also enabled me to put anxieties into perspective and to remind me of the positive aspects about myself and my world. It was these things I wanted the children I worked with to discover for themselves.

INTRODUCING MEDITATION

Before any of the children came into the room they waited at the door until I spoke to them and invited them in. They went in quietly one by one, and found a cushion to sit on in our meditation corner. I then joined them. Using cushions ensured that they had their own space. We would begin by sitting crossed-legged with our hands on our knees. They were used to sitting like this in assemblies and placing their hands on their knees ensured they were not doing anything else with them.

There was little or no conversation at this point so that everyone had time to centre themselves. Even if someone was agitated about something this would not be dealt with until after our meditation. It became apparent that often anxieties disappeared or lessened by the time we had meditated. Also the overactive, compulsive need to chat was reduced after silent meditation.

We followed this with some simple gentle stretches and loosening up of arms, necks and shoulders. We learned how we hold tension in our bodies and how we could learn to relax. Finally I asked the children to close their eyes. This is actually a very difficult thing for some children to do as they can be distrustful of other people and insecure in themselves. Knowing this I reassured them by telling them that I would have my eyes open until we were all confident and trusting as a group.

They learned, first of all, just to sit still and silent for one minute. I timed this. Some found this very hard. I ignored self-conscious giggles unless it affected other people in the group. I then gently taught them to become aware of their breath and breathing. They learned how to breathe from the bottom of their lungs and belly, experiencing the calming effect this had on them. They learned how to be aware and listen to their own breathing until they began to feel a sense of stillness and peace. In the early sessions I was keenly aware of the short attention spans most of these children had so initially meditation was just two or three minutes in duration.

It was at this point we shared our thoughts. I was amazed at the depth of thought these youngsters expressed. They showed great sympathy and empathized often with each other's experiences. We discussed bereavement, racial harassment, violence and fears with trust and compassion. I remember one boy coming into the room and curling up in the corner after his grandfather had died. We carried on and meditated and he was able to join us and speak of his grief in a room filled with people who cared deeply for him. On another occasion we learned how a boy was behaving badly because of problems at home and how we should not judge people before we know the facts. He felt able to calm down having felt he'd been listened to.

From these first steps I became aware that a huge change was happening in my work. I rarely needed to raise my voice to work effectively. There was no more rowdy thoughtlessness when the children came down to work. They began to operate as a group quicker and I was able to build a trusting working relationship within a short time of meeting them. I also found that they were ready to settle to work and keep on task better and I could speed up their work rate and self-confidence. I found that practising a variety of simple meditations, using breathing, objects and sound as ways of focusing attention before work, made us all work in a calmer, more focused and positive frame of mind.

Try for yourself, preparing your space

Small changes within the room in which you work can make a big difference: whatever you decide to try with the children you work with, make sure that you are happy with your approach. You can start off very simply with no mystique surrounding your activities. Small changes within the room in which you work can help set the kind of atmosphere you wish to create. Diffusing the light coming into the room through using muslin curtains which also shut out any other distractions, can make a huge difference. This was something often mentioned by pupils, staff and parents on entering my room.

A further addition is that of plants, flowers and other natural objects. I found these to have great significance within a city school where the seasons can change without children being aware of them. They can be used as a focus for thought and inspiration. The displays within a classroom and its layout have changed over the past few years due to the requirements of the National Curriculum. Areas have been created for maths, science and language. I feel that it is also important to create a space which may have a calming effect on pupils. A place where stillness and quiet thought can take place. Many classrooms do not lend themselves to having an area being given over to this but even a window, table or some wall space which is made special with drapes, plants, a picture, object or books can make a difference.

Creating the right atmosphere
The way you bring your pupils into the classroom sets up the atmosphere you want to create. Start off with small steps: meet your pupils at the door. While still outside your room make sure that you have their attention and that they are quiet. Let them go into the room individually or a few at a time until they are all sitting down. There may be some children you might wish to talk quietly to as they go in, reminding them of how you expect them to behave, praising their efforts, or passing on a positive comment. As the children grow used to what you expect this becomes a simple, pleasant way to come into class.

When they are sitting down try getting them to be still and quiet for one minute, actually timing this so that they get an idea of how long this actually is. (We tend to use the phrase 'just a minute' loosely but I found it helps to be precise at the outset, it works as a small challenge to some!) This helpful idea I found in Caroline Sherwood's book *Making Friends with Ourselves*.[1]

Encourage the children to shut their eyes. Remember some may find this impossible at first, so reassure them that you have your eyes open until trust is built within the class. Finish with a few deep, calming breaths. Talk them through this at first, showing them how to breathe in through the nose gently, hold, and then gently breathing out again. In Caroline Sherwood's book she suggests breathing in as if smelling a flower and gently blowing out through the mouth. Obviously you would adapt this idea to the group with which you are working.

This is enough to start with. Establish this exercise before each activity or after breaks during the day. At this point you may not have even mentioned the word 'meditation' to your class, you may just want to use this technique as a positive part of your classroom management.

HOW TO PROCEED: USING DIFFERENT MEDITATION TECHNIQUES

Let the school and parents know what you are doing and what you are trying to achieve. Introduce the class to the word 'meditation' and try different techniques. Use what works for you.

There are some misconceptions over what meditation is and its relation to religion. Some schools and parents may object to their children meditating on these grounds. Meditation is used as an important part of practice in some religions but the use of meditation as a technique in itself is now accepted as being of great benefit. Patricia Carrington in her *Learn to Meditate* kit has researched how meditation as a practical technique, unattached to any religious beliefs, can have profoundly positive effects on all who practice it.[2]

If you wish to pursue meditation with your class, discuss it with your headteacher and staff. Tell the children's parents what you are hoping to achieve and invite them in to discuss any misgivings they may have. I found that both staff and parents were supportive of my work. Some were sceptical about how it would work but were happy for me to teach their children and were pleased with the improvements in behaviour and the standard of work their children were producing as a result.

Working with the breath

This technique involves being aware of the breath. It gives focus to the children's attention. I have used it successfully with children with challenging behaviour. There is a huge amount written about the importance of breathing which can be daunting and perhaps not of relevance at a deep level when working with youngsters. We are introducing them to focusing their attention away from other distractions to their breathing, something which we all do unconsciously. Introduce them to the wonder of breathing and how it happens when we are awake and sleeping.

> The children can be sitting on the ground, on a carpet or cushions, with their legs crossed, but they might just as easily be sitting on chairs in their class places. Wherever they are, encourage them to be aware of their posture so that they are sitting with a straight back, with legs crossed if on the floor, or with both feet flat on the floor if on a chair. Ask them to place their hands on their knees.
>
> With their eyes closed, teach them to breathe in through their noses and out through their mouths. Teach them to breathe down to the bottom of their lungs and into their bellies and that breathing out slowly through their noses can be very calming. When their attention drifts away tell them to bring it back to concentrating on breathing. Build up the length of time they can sustain this. Be aware of how the children are doing and quietly guide and encourage them. The aim is to enable them to experience a sense of peace and stillness, and in this a sense of well-being.
>
> Let them sit for a few moments breathing gently before asking them to open their eyes. Ask them to keep the feeling of calm they have gained as they prepare to move on to the next class activity.

Using objects as a focus

I have used candle flames, flowers, stones and shells as a visual focus of attention. Encourage them to look closely at the chosen object. Guide them to appreciate the beauty and wonder of what is in front of them. You may need to provide more than one thing according to how many children you are working with and how they are seated. Using an object in this way can inspire children to draw wonderfully detailed and beautiful drawings. I have found working alongside children when they are doing this creates a valuable experience for the whole class, who are keen to look at your efforts as well as theirs at the end of the session.

There are structured sessions and inspiring ideas developing meditation with children in D. Rozen's book *Meditating with Children*, which you may wish to pursue.[3]

Using sound as a focus
Using sound is another way in which attention and scattered thoughts can be focused. I have used natural sounds of birds, wind and water to great effect with very lively youngsters. It can be used during meditation to enable children to find that peaceful centring we are trying to achieve, by listening mindfully to the sounds being played. I also found that after meditating many children enjoyed the gentle sounds continuing as they worked.

CONCLUSION

Simple meditation can be worked successfully into the structure of the school day, in my experience. If the children I had the privilege to work with could embrace it, then I feel sure most other children could too. I believe that simple meditation used as a means of focusing attention, and enabling peaceful reflection about the positive aspects of life and the world in which we live, can only be of benefit to those who participate. Meditation does not have to be complicated or detract from the rest of the day, indeed I believe that it can enhance the time spent in school. It is precious time well spent.

NOTES

1   Sherwood, C. (1995) *Making Friends with Ourselves*. Bath: Kidsmed.
2   Carrington, P. (1998) *Learn to Meditate* (kit). Shaftesbury: Element Books.
3   Rozen, D. (1994) *Meditating with Children*. Boulder Creek, Calif.: Planetary Publications.

CHAPTER 20

Meditation, visualization and guided imagery

Diana Grace

In this chapter we look at visualization and guided imagery, and their potential use and value in education, and how these techniques relate to meditation.

THE LINK WITH MEDITATION

Meditation is generally considered to be a focus on one thing internally, such as the breath, with eyes closed, or an external object such as a candle, with eyes open. The aim is to learn to focus on that one 'object' and to allow any other thoughts and unwanted emotions to pass by without latching on to them, thus becoming distracted by them, so that inner peace and stillness is found.

Taking the meditative process further the individual can expand their self-awareness and love to realize and experience their unity and interconnection with all things. With this heightened state of awareness the individual is able to be in the 'here and now' and to live life as a meditation, in a state of true wakefulness and compassion.

The part that visualization and guided imagery play in the process of self-awareness is far-reaching and profound, for these processes create the bridges towards that greater self-awareness. As individuals develop their imagination and ability to visualize, they realize the power of these faculties to connect to peace, beauty and strength in their hearts and minds. Also, images can be created and held in the mind's eye as a focus for meditation, such as a flower or a geometric shape such as a circle or triangle which can carry symbolic meaning. For example the circle has long been a symbol for the absolute since it has no beginning or end.

Visualization has been associated with all great meditative traditions to develop the individual's faculties of the mind and heart to align with, and be responsive to, the inner essence and source. In turn the individual's thoughts and emotions reflect that alignment through wisdom and love. The practice of visualization and guided imagery develops qualities and skills needed by the individual to grow in awareness of the deeper self, such as concentration, inward 'listening', and discipline.

VISUALIZATION

We think visually quite naturally, although we may not be conscious of this. Our image-making faculty along with our beliefs, attitudes and feelings towards self and the world determine how we experience life and create our reality of it.

Visualization or 'mental-imaging' is a skill that needs to be practised regularly in order that the ability to see clear and specific images with the mind's eye at will is developed. By introducing visualization exercises into your work with students, you are helping them to be conscious of their image-making ability so they can learn to create images that are self-empowering.

Potential uses of visualization exercises in education

Through visualization individuals can help themselves achieve their goals. These can include:

(1) strengthening positive qualities, such as love, patience and compassion;
(2) developing physical skills;
(3) relaxing and doing well in tests and exams;
(4) developing positive self-image;
(5) dealing with conflict with another person with calm and self-control.

The first images to gently nurture are positive self-images. A positive self-image is the most important asset students can have and deserves considerable attention. A positive self-image reflects the sum total of the individual's beliefs, attitudes, emotions and experience. Hence, the visualization exercises will be all the more successful where the whole school ethos supports and reinforces positive self-images and self-worth. Ideally, visualization exercises that are aimed at developing positive self-image are practised in conjunction with exploration of students' feelings and thoughts about themselves and the world during such occasions as circle time and within Personal and Social Education and Religious Education.

GUIDED IMAGERY

The terms 'guided imagery' and 'visualization' are often used interchangeably. However, for purposes of definition, whilst visualization exercises may be practised with or without guidance, a guided imagery exercise is an exercise led by the teacher. It is a guided 'inner' journey, undertaken with eyes closed, that becomes a living story for individuals as they enter into a very personal experience of it through their imagination, particularly when it is sensory oriented and images are vivid.

There have been occasions when a young child has exclaimed, 'Oh, I've been in the classroom all the time. I didn't move from here!' They have shown genuine surprise to find themselves still sitting in the circle where they started out. In one whose imagination is underdeveloped, images in the mind's eye will be vague and fleeting. With improved concentration and practice the ability to visualize is developed and images can be held for longer periods. Thus the creative potential of the journey is greatly enhanced.

Potential uses of guided imagery and visualization

A guided journey can be incorporated into any class subject to bring it to life and encourage a deeper relationship with the subject matter. This process will also encourage the development of a good memory and the individual's ability to intuit and find answers for themselves.

Teaching methods in science, for example, will be greatly facilitated with the use of guided imagery and visualization since the ability to think creatively and deal in abstractions is essential to scientific thinking. Without this capacity the student may retain information but have little or no real understanding of it. Likewise in maths, number concepts need to be grasped as well as the ability to count objects.

Guided imagery can be used to great effect to complement a class project. Students can be taken back in time to a point in history, or journey through the life cycle of a plant in science, or travel to another country and explore its landscape and culture for language or geography classes. An inner journey can be created from the theme of a favourite story or one that the class is currently exploring in English or Religious Education such as the life of a spiritual teacher. The group can be guided to meet this teacher and other characters from stories and ask their own questions of them.

During form tutor periods your class can be guided to pay attention to their inner state and move into a meditation on the breath before reviewing or previewing the day. During Personal and Social Education inner journeys can relate to the current topic, e.g. self-esteem, relationships, bullying. Imagery can be developed as a personal resource for life.

Themes for visualization and guided imagery can focus on specific values that you are exploring throughout the curriculum. All inner journeys will ideally embody spiritual values that the group can be invited to demonstrate in their relationships with people, animals and places they encounter inwardly. This will serve to help align them throughout the day with these same values and qualities.

The value of visualization and guided imagery

> The sessions are enjoyed by both pupils and staff and have a calming influence in the classroom. Improvement has been seen in the children's consideration for others, their concentration and in the use of their imagination, particularly in creative writing. (Stella Paul, Head Teacher, Charter Primary School, Wiltshire, UK)

Teachers whose students practice visualization and guided imagery have observed noticeable improvements in the following areas:

- concentration
- memory
- listening skills
- sense of responsibility and discipline
- ability to express feelings and thoughts
- ability to deal with conflict without negative physical actions
- creative and abstract thinking
- creative writing

- artwork
- calmer atmosphere
- empathy and consideration for others and the natural world.

The practice of visualization exercises and guided imagery clearly promote the development of cognitive skills (creative thinking, improved memory, concentration), yet more importantly these practices offer the individual the gift, indeed the birthright, to develop a relationship with their inner life and grow in self-love and self-worth. In turn they are able to develop a healthy self-regard, and an ability to attend to their own needs which may mean inwardly listening to and acknowledging uncomfortable feelings, rather than pushing these away as though they were terrible monsters. Through meditative practice and reflective activity the individual grows in the awareness that regardless of unwanted thoughts and feelings there is a place of beauty, love and peace inside themselves.

Potentially meditative practice, visualization and guided imagery will enhance the life of the whole school or college through creating a conducive atmosphere for the spirit of learning, and creative and harmonious relationships among teachers and students.

EXERCISES

A. Guided imagery

As with any guided journey to accompany your lesson it is helpful to start with a discussion. The following exercise can be used to accompany work that explores emotions and peace. It is suggested that 'good' feelings are primarily explored and felt in the body before the group is asked to listen inwardly to any uncomfortable feelings. Further guidance for such an exercise is included in Chapter 21, 'Introducing meditation...in early years'. Prior to embarking on this, a relaxation meditation such as attending to the breath could be followed.

Journey to a peaceful place
... Now that your body is relaxed and you are sitting with a straight back with hands in your lap, listening attentively with eyes closed to help you concentrate and see with your mind's eye, you can begin by being aware of how your body is feeling right now ... Be aware of your feet ... how do they feel? ... (Pause) ... Be aware of your legs ... how do they feel? ... (Pause) ... Be aware of your belly ... how does that feel? ... (Pause) ... be aware of your chest area ... how does that feel? ... (Pause) ... Be aware of your back ... how does that feel? ... (Pause) ... Be aware of your arms and hands ... how do they feel? ... (Pause) ... Be aware of your face and head ... how do they feel? ... (Pause) ... There may be a part of your body that is drawing your attention most ... just be present with it ... (Pause) ... *(the aim here is to encourage a shift of focus away from the chatter of the mind to feeling into the body)* ... Now ask yourself: Is there anything that is stopping me from feeling peaceful/happy/positive right now? ... (Pause) ... Allow this issue or feeling *(you may want to substitute these words for one that you are more comfortable with)* to become known to you ... and now hold it in your body, without judgement, and get a sense of where you feel it in the body ... (Pause) ... and just be present with this feeling ... it may want to express itself through memories, or words and images ... allow it to express itself to you without a judgement about it ... (Pause) ... *(this is very tricky for us because we are used to continually making judgements)* ... Now, when you are ready gently place this

issue or feeling into a basket or some other sort of container by your side ... (Pause) ... *(Repeat this process three times and leave some time for individuals to place a fourth or a fifth issue into a basket if needs be)* ... Now get a sense of how it feels to have placed these issues by your side ... (Pause) ... Go into your inner space where all is well ... and know that regardless of these issues around you now, you exist apart from them, and inside you there is peace and stillness.

You are walking down a path that is going to lead you to a peaceful place ... You decide how your path will look ... You have no shoes or socks on and you can feel the grass, or pebbles, or moss, or sand underneath your feet ... How does this feel? ... (Pause) ... Listen to the sounds around you on this path ... What do you hear? ... (Pause) ... What do you smell? ... (Pause) ... The path has now come to an end because you have arrived at your peaceful place ... Stop still and look out on this place ... it may be a place that you have visited before or a place that you are now creating ... (Pause) ... Now walk into your peaceful place, feeling the ground you are walking upon ... (Pause) ... smelling the different smells in the air ... (Pause) ... feeling the air on your face and through your hair ... (Pause) ... listening to the sounds that are here ... Find a place where you would like to be still and now sit or lie there ... (Pause) ... Just enjoy this stillness and quiet ... (Pause) ... Here the colours around you are soft and calming shades ... Here you feel you can be yourself totally ... Here you feel accepted ... Here you feel joy ... Here you feel peace ... This is a place that you can return to at any time day or night ... You may like to explore this place for a few moments or just stay where you are with your good feelings ... if you see there are friends, other people or animals here then they too have feelings of peace ... (Pause) ... Now take a moment to think of someone you would like to share your 'good' (peaceful/loving) feelings with and see them in your heart and share those feelings with them ... By your feet you now find a gift to remind you of this place ... hold it gently and place it somewhere safe ... Reach into your pocket and bring out a special gift you would like to leave here and place it somewhere ... Now give thanks for this place ... (Pause) ... it is time to leave and return to the path ... Now you are on the path again feeling the ground under your feet and walking towards the end of the path ... Now you are there ... How is your body feeling? ... Around you are your baskets with your issues or feelings inside them. Take out the first issue from its container and place it back in your body ... How does that feel now in your body? ... (Pause) ... Has anything changed? ... (Pause) ... Now place it gently into your heart centre where it will get the right attention and care it needs ... (Pause) ... *(Repeat this process for each issue)* ... In a moment we will return to class feeling relaxed, refreshed and peaceful ... When you are ready gently open your eyes.

B. Visualization

Problem solving
1. Choose three people to help you to (a) be inspired, (b) look at your situation realistically, and (c) offer you creative criticism. Draw upon your own experience of these qualities.
2. Write the word *Inspirational*, *Realist*, and *Critic*. on three pieces of A4 paper.
3. Now step onto the *'Inspirational'* paper. Relax and become still then make a mental image of the person who inspires you and become 'present' with the qualities they reflect to you. Feel these in your body. Then recall your problem or challenge and stay open and receptive to any images, ideas or answers that come to you. Follow through these same steps for *'Realist'* and *'Critic'*. Fully write insights down or share these with a partner or tutor. Students can also visualize the person who best reflects the quality they need to strengthen, and get a sense of that quality inside their body then visualize themselves expressing that quality where it is needed.

CHAPTER 21

Introducing meditation, guided imagery and visualization in early years

Diana Grace

My belief is that the key to the flowering of humanity resides in the child – as the seed of the future. By introducing meditative practice into early-years education, we are helping to facilitate a magical process of self-discovery in the child, as they enter into a relationship with their inner life and strengthen their natural sense of awe and wonder and interconnection with the world around them.

I started out in 1978 by introducing breath meditation and guided imagery to nursery school children at story time and during music and movement classes. The interest and enthusiasm for these sessions was instantaneous. As the children sat down for subsequent sessions I could see their anticipation and excitement for another personal inner adventure. I continue to observe that same exuberance and anticipation in classes both here and abroad.

Although all meditative practice can bring great benefits, there is particular value in starting young children off with a combination of breath meditation and guided imagery. These processes develop the foundation and necessary skills that will aid the child's steady self-development, self-awareness and well-being, by helping the individual to:

(1) relax,
(2) be still,
(3) concentrate,
(4) listen inwardly (to their body, feelings, thoughts and intuition),
(5) develop the image-making faculty,
(6) develop an open mind and heart,
(7) develop self-worth and self-love.

The very fact that their imagination has been engaged during a guided imagery exercise means that the young child readily makes an effort to concentrate and share about their experience and express their feelings with the class afterwards. Teachers have noticed that in the last ten years there has been a marked decline in the young child's ability to use their imagination in school. One of the first observations made by teachers who use guided imagery is that the overall creativity of the child is enhanced. Amongst the many other observed benefits of guided imagery has been the young child's ability to show empathy and consideration for others. The ability to empathize is crucial to their social and moral development.

GUIDELINES FOR THE PROCESS AND STRUCTURE OF MEDITATIVE PRACTICE WITH EARLY YEARS

The teacher: 'As teachers we are learning to respect the quiet voice of our soul, which we have often ignored' (R. R. Mukube, Head Teacher, Chimfombo Primary School, Zimbabwe). It will greatly benefit you and the children if you meditate before class, giving yourself a few minutes for stillness and centring.

Explaining aims: the youngest member of your nursery or reception class will question the reason why she is being asked to be still and quiet, whilst told to listen to a 'story' with her eyes closed! It is important to discuss in simple terms, some of the values and aims of the sessions.

Discussion and visual aids: it is important to bear in mind that young children will find it difficult to imagine and visualize places of which they have little or no direct experience. Indeed for many children that experience is limited to visiting the high street and supermarket once a week for shopping. It is helpful, then, to enter into a short discussion about the place you will be journeying to and build up a resource of visual aids, such as posters, that can support those discussions and help the children to create their own inner images.

Relaxation: relaxation is a key element in guided imagery, visualization exercises and any meditative practice. By relaxing the body the individual reaches a deeper conscious level and is able to access the farther reaches of their mind and heart and make positive changes in their emotions and thoughts. Ideally, a short relaxation exercise is practised prior to breath meditation and guided imagery.

Music: though music is not absolutely necessary, it can create a conducive atmosphere that aids the group's focus.

Close eyes: it can be a little scary for some young children to close their eyes. If this is creating a problem, then ask the child to look down to the floor until they feel comfortable enough to close their eyes.

Focus on the breath: a few minutes given to focus on breathing before moving into a guided imagery exercise, is an important part of the process. It will help children to develop the ability to be still and bring their attention to the present moment, as well as offering an opportunity for enjoying silence and relaxation and a sense of harmony with self and others.

GUIDED IMAGERY

Guided imagery provides you, the facilitator, with an opportunity to follow your own inner creativity and intuition by allowing the journey to spontaneously unfold. By guiding the journey in this way you will find that you become responsive to the needs of your class in that particular moment.

Initially you may want to build up your own confidence by following a script that you have adapted for your class, or you may want to play a recorded journey. Ideally you will have spent time learning to facilitate simple forms of meditative practice for young people with someone who has a background experience in this field. Although guided imagery can be used to complement your class projects, it is also suggested that the class has an opportunity to choose the theme of their journey.

Guidelines for guided imagery

Timing: timing depends on various factors, the energy levels of the class, and how long they have been accustomed to meditative practice. You may want to keep the session to ten minutes, although you will find that when your class become very absorbed in the journey they can go on for longer periods.

Speak in the present tense: by speaking in the present tense the group becomes focused in the 'here and now' and this helps to keep their imagination and visualization vivid.

Pauses: it is helpful to leave pauses and times for silence in your guided imagery, so the group can explore what they wish, or can simply 'be' and experience stillness or a quality such as joy.

Imaginary vehicles or gadgets: incorporating fun imaginary gadgets or magical vehicles to take the children to their destinations is one successful way to help boys in particular to concentrate and participate more fully in the session.

Use all the senses: in both guided imagery and visualization exercises it is important to involve all the senses. In the world of sport, for example, where it has been long recognized that the mind and emotions influence physical performance, visualization with a strong kinaesthetic component is widely practised.

Important reminders: it is important to remind the group that whosoever they meet or whatsoever places they visit are always friendly, safe and peaceful.

Abstract concepts, such as 'Feel there is a circle of pink loving light around you', can be too difficult for young children to grasp and are best not used.

Being accompanied on the journey: younger children respond well to having a friend accompany them on their journey. This could be someone of their choosing such as an imaginary animal friend, or a cuddly toy that you create a particular character for and whom they meet on each journey.

Gifts: children always enjoy receiving a special imaginary gift from a friend they have made on their inner journey. These can be explored and placed somewhere safe. They might also pick up a natural object from the places they visit and bring these back to class, as a souvenir. They will also enjoy giving a gift to someone on their journey.

Heart focus: it works well to integrate a heart focus into the journey towards the end or as an exercise in itself. Young children will readily relate to being asked to focus on an image of a person or a family pet they love, which they can then place in their heart area of their body. They can then be asked to feel the warmth of the feelings in their heart, before being led to give thanks to their loved one and a big hug. Their love can be extended to many others, e.g. members of the group that are absent, the group as a whole and the wider community in which they live.

Returning back to class: it works well to finish the guided journey by leading the group back to the classroom along the same route they took to arrive at a particular place. Then guide them to gently open their eyes and enjoy a few moments of silence before your feedback and sharing.

By facilitating the experience of meditative practice, visualization and guided imagery for the child, you are attending to their heart and soul as well as their mind. You are contributing to their lives in some of the most positive ways open to you. You will be planting precious seeds that will bear fruit in many shapes and sizes, not least of all personal resources for life.

I was greatly encouraged when questioning one of the classes I had introduced these practices to, four years previously, whilst they were in year one. The majority of the class remembered the sessions in great detail and which of the guided journeys they had enjoyed most. Fifty per cent of the group said they still use the techniques they were taught when they feel the need, such as at home before sleeping, prior to a school test, or a performance in a school play.

EXERCISES

Breath meditation
It is a good idea, at some point, that the group is encouraged to reflect on the blessing of air and our interdependence with the environment through breathing. Moreover, the act of breathing is a common activity we share with all life forms. Start with a short relaxation exercise:

Check that the group have good posture (relaxed shoulders and spine, neck and head pointed in same direction).

Check that they are taking complete even breaths (so they will feel their belly moving slightly out as they breathe in and in as they breathe out).

... Now that your body is well relaxed ... take nice even breaths into your body and feel your belly moving slightly out as you breathe in ... and feel it moving slightly in when you breathe out ... (Pause) ... Follow the air in through your nostrils ... and all the way down into your body ... and follow it out again ... (Pause) ... feeling the air cool as you breathe it in ... and feeling its warmth as it flows back out ... (Pause) ... (Repeat) ... If you notice yourself thinking about other things gently bring your attention back to your breathing ... in through your nostrils and feeling the warm air flowing back out ... Just continue focusing on the natural rhythm of your breath ... in and out ... (Now be silent for a few minutes before you lead the group to open eyes, or follow through with a guided imagery exercise.)

The aim of the following exercise is to help the child connect to their feelings inside their body and listen to the 'body's story'. By learning to be aware of the loving and caring feelings inside them, the child can be guided to have gentle and caring feeling towards uncomfortable and scary feelings, rather than push these aside. By listening inwardly and acknowledging fear as well as love, the child learns to be comfortable with herself and so releases the tension in her body. At the same time by guiding the child into a journey where they experience peace and beauty they learn and find strength from knowing that regardless of uncomfortable thoughts or emotions there is still peace and love inside them.

This exercise is best done after your group is well acquainted with meditative practice.

Prior to this exercise have your class bring in cuddly toys or pictures or photos of cuddly animals, or cuddly toys.

'The body's story'

Exercise A:
1. Ask children to reflect on how a cuddly toy or animal (this could be their pet) makes them feel. Ask them to imagine holding that animal or toy.
2. Brainstorm on words to describe those feelings, i.e. cosy, snugly, loving, caring.
3. Ask children to close their eyes and get a sense of where these feelings are inside their body. (The group will generally locate those feelings in the heart.)
4. Give an opportunity for the group to share their reflections.
5. Then take the group on a guided journey to experience those loving feelings with their cuddly toy or pet.
6. Allow time for sharing.
   Create a display or poster with all the contributions of pictures and words from the brainstorm. This can be used for reference and further discussion, in your next session, as you take the process further.

Exercise B:
1. Recap on the last session and remind the group about their loving and caring feelings inside them.
2. Discuss uncomfortable feelings and ask the group, 'Are there any uncomfortable feelings that sometimes stop you from feeling the loving and caring feelings inside?'
3. Brainstorm on words to describe those feelings.
4. Now ask the group to close their eyes and ask, 'Is there anything right now that might stop you from feeling as loving and caring as you can be?'
5. Ask the group to get a sense of where they might feel any uncomfortable feelings in their body and place their hand there and just hold those feelings in a caring way as they might hold a small pet.
   Suggest that they might see pictures or words that come up as they hold those uncomfortable feelings. Guide the group to just look at these and carry on holding the feeling in a caring way.
6. Ask the group, when they feel ready, to place these uncomfortable feelings in an imaginary basket or box by their side.
   Here remind the children that regardless of uncomfortable feelings they also have loving, caring and peaceful feelings inside.
7. Take the group on a short guided journey to be with their loved pets or cuddly toys or to a peaceful place. The guided journey 'Peaceful Place' in Chapter 20 has been designed as a body-feel exercise and can be adapted for early years. It is important that the group place their uncomfortable feelings back into their body as suggested in 'Peaceful Place'.

CHAPTER 22

Christian meditation in the classroom

Sheela Valavi

In a world that is growing increasingly aware of its need for stability and depth, meditation is a spiritual tradition found at the heart of every religion, including Christianity, speaking to increasing numbers of contemporary men and women. It is a path beyond thought and imagination into the indwelling presence within our hearts. The way is one of simplicity and discipline, and down through the centuries people have sought teachers to inspire them and communities of fellow-pilgrims with whom to journey. The foundation of Christian meditation has been inspired by the work of one such teacher, John Main, a Benedictine monk (1926–82), who in 1975 rediscovered a simple tradition of silent contemplative prayer in the manner of the Desert Fathers – early Christian monks living in the Egyptian Desert following a life of solitary prayer.

The essence of meditation is taking the attention off ourselves and looking forward, beyond ourselves, into the mystery of God; of travelling beyond ourselves into His love, into union. Meditation is a way that brings every part of our day, all our experience and all the dimensions of our being, into harmony. It is the way beyond the personal dividedness and anxiety from which we suffer as a result of our denial of God and our separation from the Spirit.

HOW TO MEDITATE

> Sit down in a comfortable position, the spine upright. Sit still; close your eyes gently. Say your mantra MA-RA-NA-THA. Four equally stressed syllables. Say it with loving attention of the heart. For students, you may also use a word that is comfortable, like Jesus, Abba (Father), Peace, or Love. Empty your minds of any thoughts or images. If you stop saying your mantra, return to it and keep returning to it. Meditation is a challenge and discipline. The challenge is to let go of ourselves and simply place ourselves in the mystery of God. Begin meditating for twenty minutes, slowly lengthening to thirty minutes.
>
> For students, begin meditating for five to ten minutes, slowly lengthening the time.

Maranatha means 'Come Lord'. It is an Aramaic word. The power of the mantra begins not just to sound in our head, but in our hearts. The coming together brings harmony to the complete being. It is the faith that makes this meditation Christian.

The mantra is a way of kenosis (conversion), an emptying of egoism that leads to fullness of being. There is shift of consciousness through meditation. In meditation we go beyond ego to our true self. John Main speaks about our true self and the need of 'smashing the mirror' of our ego. When we are united to God 'as our supreme power source', we break through the mirror of the 'hyper-self-consciousness' of egoism.[1] In meditation our 'egoism', or the false self, melts slowly away as the focus of attention shifts from self to God and then to others.

Why does this happen? The saying of the mantra is an act of pure selflessness. Each time we say our mantra we renounce and leave behind 'my' own thoughts, 'my' own words, 'my' own concerns, 'my' own fears, and 'my' own anxieties. In losing these selfish possessions we begin to lose the false self. In this detachment, which meditation requires, the mask is stripped away to reveal where the true 'I' has been hiding.

Silence is the first requisite for listening

Speaking to Italian teachers, Pope John Paul II mentioned that the first attitude to develop in students is attention, and continued: 'this requires that you help your students not to suffocate but rather to nourish their innate amazement in the face of creation and to reflect on it in order to grasp its perfection'.[2] To educate to this attitude, it is indispensable that the child be led to a real and profound interior *silence* which is the first requisite for listening.

Silence is to be understood primarily as interior, the calming of the mind's noise and an awakening to the silent presence of our Creator within. If seen as an interior reality, silence leads not to escape from, or evasion of, the world but to a deeper involvement in it.

In silence you are not playing a role or fulfilling any expectations. You are just there, realizing your being, open to reality. Then, in the Christian vision, you are overwhelmed by the discovery that the reality in which we have our being is love. In silence we know that our spirit is expanding into love.

To learn to be silent is to begin a journey. All you have to do is to begin. To take the first step into the silence is to begin the journey of your life, the journey into life. You are learning two things: firstly, to sit still, not because you are afraid to move or are imposing a burden on yourself, but because in stillness you seek a unity of body, mind and spirit. Secondly, to recite your mantra in response to the deepening silence that arises in stillness.

As you begin to say your mantra you become aware that you are on the threshold of silence. This is a critical moment for most people, as they leave the familiar world of sounds, ideas, thoughts, words and images. You do not know what is in store for you as you cross into the silence. This is why it is so important to learn to meditate in a tradition and in a group that receives, passes on and embodies that tradition. It is for us a tradition that says 'fear not'.

Posture

Sit with your spine upright: sit down, either on the floor or in an upright chair, and keep your spine as erect as possible. Close your eyes gently. Stillness in meditation leads to the knowledge of God through the integration of body and mind in the higher unity of the spirit.

Simplicity
Simplicity is the most difficult because it involves the unfolding of consciousness from its habitual doing (practising or acting in some manner by force of habit), from its self-conscious and self-reflective state, into a natural transcendence, purity of heart, and peace.

WAYS INTO MEDITATION
There are many ways of leading students into meditation, e.g. games, relaxation exercises, self-awareness exercises or listening to peaceful music.

> *Breathing*: become aware of the air as it comes in and goes out through your nostrils. Become aware of the warmth or coldness of the air ... its coldness when it comes in, its warmth when it goes out. Limit your awareness to the air. Be sensitive and alert to the slightest, lightest touch of the air on your nostrils as you inhale and exhale ... Stay with this awareness for five minutes.
>
> *Self-awareness*: take a comfortable position. Go over the whole of your body, starting with the top of your head and ending with the tips of your toes. Be aware of every sensation in each part. If any part of your body is tense, stay on that for a few seconds. Once again, move from head to foot for five minutes.
>
> *Stand* straight and raise your hands till they are stretched out in front of you, parallel to the floor ... now open them out wide in the form of an embrace ... Hold this posture for a minute. Rest and then repeat the gesture.

Students may feel foolish, or afraid of peer pressure. This leads to giggling or silliness. The best way of overcoming this is to tell the students beforehand that this is normal and no one is going to take any notice or be affected by it. Do not try to measure your progress. If you need to access results, ask yourself how much more loving you are in your relationships with others.

Challenges
The first shock awaiting beginner meditators is the discovery of just how busy their minds are. The human mind can be described as being like a tree full of monkeys, jumping from one branch to another, screaming and chattering away. We are thinking about the future, we are thinking about the past, we are in fantasy and daydreams. In fact, we are everywhere except here and now which is where meditation aims to bring us.

For the teacher
When questioning the students about their difficulties, worries and anxieties, start where they are. Breathing exercises will help them to calm down, playing music at the beginning of meditation leads the students into silence. A great source of wonder is science and the natural world. This leads them again into a profound silence at the source of being.

Take a bit of time to think about the medium through which you express yourself most easily; this will be the one to build on in your story-telling. What moves you most? Is it nature or music? Literature art or drama? Science or the great outdoors? Somewhere inside you is a key to good story-telling and if you can find it, it will liberate you as well as your students. In the context of meditation, it can lead both you and them into the silence.

FRUITS OF MEDITATION

With children
They come to know themselves better. Children become more peaceful. Their power of concentration increases. They are able to relate better with other people. Their quality of life improves. The purpose of meditating is to advance along the way to the fullness of your own humanity. Children discover that they have a purpose in their life. They begin to see meaning in life. Love grows in their heart.

With adults
The wonderful thing we discover as we meditate is that there is only one centre, and that centre is everywhere, and that meditation is the way of being linked to it in our own centre. We are able to be in harmony with anyone and everyone.

Meditation brings one into unity with self, mind, body, spirit and emotions. It develops a spirit of forgiveness beginning to heal the emotional hurts of our early childhood. The shadow side of the psyche begins to heal. Some people have a deep resentment toward their mother or father. They harbour deep resentment arising from neglect, maltreatment and sometimes even sexual abuse. These are wounds in the psyche and they continue to afflict us unless they are released from our unconscious. The healing of these hurts take place through the discipline of the mantra.

In meditation we come to an experiential conviction that we are loved by another person, profoundly loved. We understand deeply that it is not that I love but that I am loved. Through this acceptance of the gift of love, we grow from childhood to adulthood.

In the silence of meditation God reaches down into the depths and liberates us little by little from the emotional damage of a lifetime. There is an organic unfolding, in its own time, of our buried neurosis.

In meditation our pain is identified and brought into the light. The healing process of Christian meditation can then begin. This is a path that leads from brokenness to wholeness. How do we know we are healed? We can recognize this when the recurring reactions related to the pain have disappeared and the recollection of the traumatic events, whether it be expressed or not, leaves not even a trace of painful or lasting sensations of any kind.

When we meditate we enter into a relationship with all. We start to recognize and understand with clarity of consciousness what is going on at a much deeper level. As we learn to meditate, we recognize the richness within, and the sacredness of each living creature, and the role that each has. When we share the silence of our meditation together, each of us is transformed as we travel within and beyond ourselves and we each and all of us, in a Christian sense, become one in Him.

Medical evidence shows that meditation lowers blood pressure and enhances the immune system. But the greatest significance of meditation is enhancing the sense of our human wholeness in the harmony of body, mind and spirit. Meditation, in essence, is a way of learning to become awake, fully alive and yet still.

NOTES

1   See John Main (1999) *Moment of Christ*. London: Medio Media.
2   Pope John Paul II, Address to participants at the National Congress of the Italian Association of Catholic Teachers, 6 December 1984.

CHAPTER 23

Meditation in collective worship and circle time

Nicky Newton

CIRCLE TIME AS A FRAMEWORK FOR COLLECTIVE WORSHIP

The legal requirement for a daily act of collective worship 'wholly or mainly of a broadly Christian character' in a pluralistic and increasingly secular society presents a considerable challenge for many schools. Children and staff do not necessarily come from practising Christian backgrounds, and within any school community there will be representatives from a variety of religious and non-religious backgrounds. In addition, worship is essentially a voluntary activity and cannot be compelled. Circle time and meditation can make a valuable contribution to the worship programme of a school, respecting the integrity of individual members of the community whilst continuing to provide a shared experience of worship.

When introducing these activities it is important that a school has clearly defined the essential elements of worship. If we use the Qualifications and Curriculum Authority's (QCA) definition, worship should provide opportunities for developing a sense of the transcendent, pondering ultimate questions, reflecting on the meaning and purpose of life, exploring religious ideas, celebration and learning from others.[1] Whilst it should be daily it does not have to always be a gathering of the whole school, it can include key stage and class groupings. If a worship programme is varied it will retain the interest of individual pupils and be easily tailored to the needs of individual age groups. The inclusion of meditation and circle time within worship is particularly valuable when used with smaller groupings such as classes.

The techniques of circle time as a structured time where a class group meets in a circle to speak, listen, reflect and interact provide a clear framework for a class act of worship which includes meditation. It provides clear ground rules for interaction which ensures that the views of all class members are respected, it provides a forum for discussion, encourages a sense of group identity but most importantly provides physical and temporal space for reflection. Circle time is deceptively simple to introduce. At its most basic level it involves the whole class, including the teacher, sitting in a circle and discussing issues of importance. If it is to be used effectively, however, it is important that it is carefully structured and managed by the teacher initially. Circle time should happen regularly to allow the children to develop the skills and confidence to use the time effectively. Clear ground rules should be established and reviewed regularly by the whole group and the teacher should also abide by these rules. The time itself should be well planned with a range of interactive games and stimuli for discussion, and there are a wide range of resources published to help with this, examples of which are listed in the resources section at the end of this book.

SIMPLE GUIDELINES FOR SUCCESSFUL CIRCLE TIME

(1) Prepare well in advance;
(2) ensure that circle time is not interrupted;
(3) agree the ground rules as a group;
(4) encourage turn taking in discussion by passing round a special object – only the group member holding the object has the right to speak;
(5) value all contributions – make sure no contributions are put down by other group members;
(6) keep the atmosphere positive;
(7) make it fun and light-hearted – though you will be discussing issues of importance, circle time should not be too heavy;
(8) start a game to break the ice – see the resource list for suggestions;
(9) have a clear ending with concrete outcomes, i.e. brainstorm the qualities of a good friend, draw up a strategy of what to do if you see someone being bullied;
(10) don't force pupils to contribute.

Circle time is essentially concerned with social development and will only constitute an act of worship if religious content and religious activities are included. To become an act of worship it should encourage an atmosphere of reverence and provide opportunities for reflection and response. The techniques of meditation enable individuals to reflect on those things which have meaning and worth for them. It is a spiritual activity which has roots within a variety of religious traditions including Christianity. To be used in class worship it needs to be within a framework which enables individual reflection whilst retaining the group identity. Circle time can provide the framework, whilst meditation the religious/Christian focus.

PRACTICAL CONSIDERATIONS

Setting it up
It is important that the classroom has a different feel for worship so that the children are able to appreciate that this time is a special time and not just another lesson. The room should be arranged in such a way as to encourage reverence, stillness and a sense of community. This can be difficult because space is limited and it is not always practical or possible to rearrange furniture. If possible the children should be sat in a circle either on the carpet or in their chairs. Ensure that all equipment is put away, making sure that the children have nothing to fiddle with. Have a focus which pupils will learn to recognize and respect – candle, vase of flowers, cross picture, sculpture,

natural object, open Bible. This should be brought out for worship/meditation and not be left on display at other times. It will provide a visual focus for meditation and contribute to an atmosphere of reverence and 'specialness'.

The setting up of the room can act as a valuable opening/closing routine designed to lead the children into and out of worship. It can set the boundaries and enable the teacher to set an appropriate tone.

Timing

Little and often is best to begin with. Initially, ten minutes will be appropriate but you may wish to extend this time as the children become more skilled in worship. There should be a regular planned time slot. When you are identifying the time think about the following:

1. What will the other classes around be doing? Leading quiet mediation in your classroom while drama is happening next door can be difficult. If you overlook a field/playground, pupils can be very distracted watching another class doing PE. You cannot avoid every distraction but you can minimize them. Teaching children to tune out distraction should be an entering-in activity, and initially will be an important part of the programme.

2. What will come before/after worship? Will worship be a response to some aspect of the curriculum? Will it be a start of the day's activity or an ending? Will it be followed by a creative activity? The meditation may be structured to lead out of or into another activity.

3. How will the meditation fit into the rhythm of the school day? Will it be following a period of activity such as break, lunch, arrival at school or PE or will it be following a period of concentration such as literacy hour?

Content

The structure and style may vary but the following elements should be included:

Opening/closing activity: children need to understand that this is a special time. The opening and closing activities set the boundaries, they enable the teacher to set an appropriate tone. Setting up the room and putting the room back together can be a useful way of drawing the children into and out of the special time. I have found it helpful to use the same routine entering in and coming out: this reinforces the sense of specialness/apartness of the time set aside. The tone can be set by the playing of appropriate music throughout.

Begin by packing away equipment and rearranging seating. Once the class is settled have an established routine for bringing out the focus, e.g. lighting the candle, putting a special object reflecting the theme on the table, opening a Bible. You may wish to use some verbal response. Liturgical responses such as

Teacher: peace be with you,
Children: and also with you,

are particularly useful and can be adapted to suit a variety of situations. In this case the word peace can be replaced by a variety of alternatives (love, joy, hope) depending on the theme.

Reflection: introducing meditation: this element will act as the focus for the worship and can include a wide range of meditative activities. Guided meditations based on stories can be a very effective way of engaging children with spiritual material and encouraging them to explore their own perspectives. This particular form of meditation is based on the Ignation method of praying with the Gospels. In its simplest form this involves taking a gospel scene and trying to 'make it present' through the use of the imagination. This example is based upon the story of Jesus and Zacchaeus. Before beginning the meditation the teacher should briefly introduce the theme and relate it to the everyday experience of the pupils. She should then begin the meditation with an entering-in exercise such as 'tuning in the radio' or encouraging pupils to focus on their own breathing.

Imagine that you have travelled back in time to the time of Jesus. You are in the city of Jericho. It is very hot, feel the sun on your skin ... Look around you, what is it like? ... What do the houses look like? ... What are the people wearing? ... What can you see happening?

You become aware of a large crowd gathering. They are very excited because they are expecting a very important visitor. Listen to what they are saying ... Watch them gathering at the side of the road ... In the distance you notice a very short man trying to get a view. No one seems to like him. They keep pushing him away, shutting him out ... look at his face. How do you think he feels? Is he happy or upset? Why do you think he is upset? You wonder why no one likes him? You hear he is a tax collector and has been stealing from people. What do you think about this? ... You see the little man climb up a tree.

The visitor is arriving ... everyone starts cheering. You see it is Jesus. Before you can get a good look you see him walk up to the tree and look at the little man. You hear him say 'Hurry down Zacchaeus, because I want to come to your house for tea.' The crowd are angry, what do they say? ... The little man is very excited because it is the first time someone has been nice to him in a long time ... you hear him promise to give back all he has stolen ... You are so busy watching Zacchaeus that you don't notice Jesus walking towards you. He is standing next to you. What does he say ...?

You may wish to read the story to the class before doing the meditation, then discuss its main themes afterwards, e.g. including outsiders, helping everyone, not judging people on external appearances but get to know them better. Allow pupils an opportunity to reflect upon their own experiences related to the theme, drawing out the ideas that have significance for them, based on the experience of the guided meditation. It might be appropriate to ask the pupils to think about certain questions and experiences. What makes a good friend? An occasion when they have felt excluded and what helped them cope, or a time when they were given, or have given someone else, a second chance.

This example has used explicitly Christian material, it is equally possible to use material from other faith traditions or none. Many of the 'moral' stories found in traditional assembly books can be adapted for meditation and it is important that the teacher selects material that is relevant to the age and backgrounds of the pupils.[2]

Response
This is an important part of the worship experience. It draws the pupils back into the classroom. It enables pupils to share their experience if they choose

to, learning from each other's experience. Most importantly it encourages pupils to apply what they have learnt from their meditation to their everyday lives. It can take many forms and it is important that there is no sense of compulsion. Activities used may include:

(1) prayers of intercession either taken from the Christian tradition, from collections of prayers or produced by the class or individuals. Appropriate liturgical prayers may include the Lord's Prayer, the Prayer of St Francis, or the prayer of confession from the ASB service book;
(2) a hymn or song appropriate to the theme;
(3) discussion followed by a concrete act of commitment such as a brainstorm of possible actions, or each pupil writing an intention on a piece of paper. This paper can then be kept, shared with others or added to a class display.

NOTES

1 SCAA (1995) *Spiritual and Moral Development*, Discussion Paper No. 3. London: School Curriculum and Assessment Authority. Subsequently, SCAA changed its name to the Qualifications and Curriculum Authority.
2 A useful resource is Margaret Cooling (1990) *Assemblies for Primary Schools*. ACT (Association of Christian Teachers), and Norwich, RMEP (Religious and Moral Education Press).

CHAPTER 24

Meditation and holistic education: the way forward

Clive Erricker

This chapter acts as a conclusion to the book and places meditation in the context of holistic education. We live in grim educational times. In my experience of speaking with teachers on INSET courses and in schools I have met an overwhelming sense of disappointment and frustration at the lack of time available and attention paid to the larger aims of education and the pupil as a person. At the same time I have attended, and sometimes spoken at, conferences addressing the same aims. The disparity of view encountered is quite remarkable. Whilst those who represent government initiatives, through the Qualifications and Curriculum Authority (QCA) and Teacher Training Agency (TTA), speak of improvements in efficiency and achievement, teachers speak of a lack of time to address their pupils' development beyond the prescriptions set for curriculum attainment targets, and of a fatigue in their own practice due to increased documentation requirements. So, who is right? One cannot overcome this disparity without delving deeper into the purposes of education.

PURPOSES OF EDUCATION

If one asks whether imagination, reflection, well-being, etc. are important in education both teachers and those who represent government agencies will emphatically agree that they are. Yet, in practice, this does not appear to be the case. We have to place such terms within different frameworks of educational meaning. Whilst no one, within any educational service, will deride such qualities, hierarchically they are given less attention *for their own sake* once specific skills, competencies and curriculum knowledge targets are identified as of prime importance. Schools that do not achieve sufficiently in relation to the latter will fail inspection. However, they can also fail in other areas, e.g. spiritual development, if they do not attend to the former. In practice, the resolution of such a conundrum invariably resides in the question of where the school is situated and what constitutes its intake. Social deprivation is the key issue that tends to divide schools and children that succeed from those that fail or just scrape through. Whilst social deprivation is intimately linked with economic deprivation, a condition of scarcity in financial terms, it is the effect of both educational and emotional deprivation in the first instance.

Schools in which I have worked can be divided into those which were reaching out for some further specialist input to deal with their children's problems, and those which wished to provide extra enrichment for their children. Generally speaking, the former were happy to give whatever time was necessary to attending to their children's basic human needs, the latter were seeking to provide an efficiently delivered 'extra' to their children's education. What I have done has been received differently in each case. Introducing meditation and other calming and reflective techniques into a school's provision can be a rewarding extra, or it can provide an opportunity to reconceive the basis of its educational vision. When children are asked to attend to their 'whole selves', reflect on their experiences and act on the basis of that reflection it does not result in conformity but questioning. Children become empowered and seek to act on that feeling of empowerment to change things in their lives, to cope on their own terms, to put into effect their own vision of achievement. This can be uncomfortable for schools, teachers and parents. Children become their own persons. This sounds like education, but unfortunately it is the very thing that education often tries to repress (though that would never be said).

Of course, we can start to see the obviousness of this outcome when we identify those historical figures who provide the template for it. Jesus, the Buddha, Muhammad, Che Guevara, Martin Luther King, Gandhi and numerous others are precisely the revolutionary figures who have spoken and acted according to an empowerment that was based upon their own experiences and the convictions that followed. We either domesticate their consumption by children, such that it results in a tendency towards conformity, or ostracize them from our curriculum, due to the heretical nature of their pronouncements. Either way, it is a form of social control. The authentic voice, insofar as we are able to access it, is silenced. The same is true for children.

The expectation of conformity has a deep residual impact. When I first went to university it dawned on me, during my first year, that I could think what I liked. This did not mean I could do what I liked; but for the first time I consciously voiced to myself that understanding. It led me, in subsequent years, to ask why I first became aware of that possibility at such a late age (twenty in my case). Subsequently again, it informed my professional practice in schools and higher education. In retrospect, it has been the guiding criterion for my own professional practice, insofar as I have been able to put it into effect. A result of this has been to seek to ensure that the individuals I have taught recognize this possibility for themselves as an immediate priority. Without this recognition their educational development will be impoverished, or even retarded.

Meditation is a key strategy in ensuring those in institutionalized education recognize their potential. It is concerned with reflecting upon one's own experience without being caught up in the anxieties, prejudices and attachments that construe our motivations and pronouncements according to our own gain or desires. It is, therefore, a way of promoting constructive contributions to educational, social and community debate. At the same time, it results in individuals speaking with confidence and conviction, a felt knowledge of what is appropriate to be voiced, whether or not it leads to consensus or opposition. As a result, it is not a comfortable educational option. The empowerment of pupils leads to the requirement of negotiation, not control. But, at the same time, what is voiced is of importance and not peripheral to the concerns of the school community and its members.

HOLISTIC EDUCATION

Holistic education is an umbrella term that can easily be put to different instrumental uses. I wish to identify its sufficiency in relation to meditation, as an empowering practice to achieve our human potential, and in relation to the educational need to ensure that individuals develop with regard to all their faculties: cognitive, affective and physical. Here I can offer an example in relation to my own family experience. My son was largely disaffected with his own educational experience. Having studied in school and sixth-form college he found little to excite his interest. Yet, at the age of seventeen, he discovered Kung Fu. His orientation progressively changed. He deepened his interest in ideas that this martial art was based on, he attended to the relationship between bodily action, mental discipline and harmonious relationships. His ownership of this development of his potential was not without changes in our family structure, or even the configurations of space occupied in our house and garden. Negotiation of needs and requirements became a significant feature of family discussion, as did the financing of pursuing a particular interest by means of employment. Change in and development of orientation required significant social negotiation, but from a base of commitment and responsibility. In his own way our son took responsibility for his own holistic development as a person. Thus, he educated himself through ownership of his own life and its prospects in a sense that was never apparent before. This induced respect.

The above example is of a particular kind, but the general principles can be applied in numerous situations, in school and family contexts. In a more professional role, in my research and that of the research project of which I am a part,[1] the same issues have emerged. In speaking to children in primary school about their lives, experiences, needs and concerns they have voiced issues that are rarely addressed in the educational domain, and often not elsewhere in their lives. These voices are indicative of the need to both take children's reflections seriously and to ensure we communicate with them educationally as part of our professional duties. Otherwise we do not actually know the person who is being educated and what they are learning, in that larger domain of attitudes and values. I include, below, examples of children speaking from their experience. In relation to this it should become evident the role meditation, as a dispassionate reflection on experience, can play in taking education forward, and the potential young people have for meditative practice.

Bradley, who is seven, shows us how the imagination can create a sense of the presence of those whom he wishes to remember. It is a form of untutored visualization that he uses to deal with separation. Zek speaks of his experience of meditating in a special unit in school, in order to control his agressive behaviour, and the benefits of doing it.

Bradley's story

I like playing on the swings in the park. It feels like a rocket going backwards and forwards up on the air. I like playing on the trees as well. The swings are different if you shut your eyes. If you shut your eyes on the swing it feels scary. It's black and it looks like you're in space. Sometimes it feels like I'm going to Scotland on my swing – whoosh! And then when I get to Scotland I'm going to look for my brother.

When I'm in a special place I like to think of special people, even though they're not there, like I think of my brother in Scotland, even though he's not there.

Zek's story

My name is Zek ... I am 12 years old ... We start each day ... with a little bit of meditation. It helps me at the unit, home and even at school. My mom thinks I am a lot calmer at home ... At school when I am getting told off I feel like saying things like shut up but at the unit they teach you to think it in your head but do not say it ... I hope I can continue to do this when I get angry.

IN CONCLUSION

Meditation and education can be understood as two terms foreign to each other, practices carried out in different worlds, or intimately connected such that the terms are almost interchangeable. If we read the following quotation from Krishnamurti and then replace the term 'meditation' by 'education', it may present both in a new light:

> What is important in meditation is the quality of mind and heart ... meditation is not a means to an end. It is both the means and the end ... If there is no meditation, then you are like a blind man in a world of great beauty, light and colour.[2]

Similarly, if we read the following observation by the French anthropologist Claude Lévi-Strauss, not a Buddhist or a religious man, it may make us wonder why we have ignored meditation in education for so long (but that would be another story!):

> what have I learned from the masters I have listened to, the philosophers I have read, the societies I have investigated, and that very science in which the West takes such pride? Simply a fragmentary lesson or two which, if laid end to end, would add up to the meditations of the Sage at the foot of his tree.[3]

NOTES

1 The Children and Worldviews Project. A report on our research into children's narratives and the implications for education can be found in Erricker, C., Erricker, J., Ota, C., Sullivan, D., and Fletcher, M. (1997) *The Education of the Whole Child*. London: Cassell. Also consult our website: *www.cwvp.ucc.ac.uk*.
2 Krishnamurti, J. (1973) *The Only Revolution*. Mary Lutyens (ed.), London: Gollancz, p. 14.
3 Quoted in M. Carrithers (1983) *The Buddha*. Oxford: Oxford University Press, pp. 1–2.

Part 4:

Resources

If not easily available locally, suggested books can be ordered through the following bookshops which specialize in books on meditation, spirituality and religion. In other instances specific addresses are given.

Watkins Bookshop, 21 Cecil Court, London WC2N 4EZ
Tel: 0207 836 2182, Fax: 0207 836 6700
Compendium Books, 234 Camden High Street, London NW1 8QS
Tel. 0207 485 8944, Fax: 0207 267 0193

1. Meditation and Meditation with Children

Beesley, M. (1990) *Stilling: A Pathway for Spiritual Learning in the National Curriculum.* Salisbury: Salisbury Diocesan Board of Education.

Beesley, M. (1992) *Space for the Spirit.* Salisbury: Salisbury Diocesan Board of Education.

Benson, H. (1975) *The Relaxation Response.* New York: Avon Books.

Benson, H. (1984) *Beyond the Relaxation Response.* New York: Time Books.

Carrington, P. (1977) *Freedom in Meditation.* Garden City, NY: Anchor Press.

Carrington, P. (1998) *Learn to Meditate* (kit – cassettes). Available from Element Books, The Old School House, The Courtyard, Bell Street, Shaftesbury, Dorset SP7 SPB.

Carrington, P. (1998) *The Book of Meditation: The Complete Guide to Modern Meditation.* Shaftesbury: Element Books.

Claxton, G. (1997) *Hare Brain, Tortoise Mind.* London: Fourth Estate.

Day, J. (1994) *Creative Visualization with Children.* Shaftesbury: Element Books.

Fontana, David (1991) *The Elements of Meditation.* Shaftesbury: Element Books.

Fontana, David (1992) *The Meditator's Handbook.* Shaftesbury: Element Books.

Fontana, D. and Slack, I. (1997) *Teaching Meditation to Children: A Practical Guide to the Use and Benefits of Basic Meditation Techniques.* Shaftesbury: Element Books.

Fuggit, E. (1983) *He Hit Me Back First.* Calif.: Jalman Press; New York: Routledge.

Hewitt, James (1988) *Teach Yourself Relaxation.* Sevenoaks: Hodder & Stoughton.

Hewitt, James (1992) *Teach Yourself Yoga.* Sevenoaks: Hodder & Stoughton.

Kabat-Zinn, Jon (1994) *Mindfulness Meditation: Wherever You Go There You Are.* London: Piatkus; New Leaf: USA.

Kabat-Zinn, Jon (1994) *Mindfulness Meditation: Wherever You Go There You Are.* Practice tapes, London: Piatkus, Also available from Stress Reduction Tapes, PO Box 547, Lexington, Mass. 02173 USA; and New Leaf: USA.

Langer, Ellen J. (1997) *The Power of Mindful Learning.* Reading, Mass.: Addison-Wesley.

Le Shan, L. (1975) *How to Meditate.* New York: Bantam Books.

Levete, Gina (1987) *Presenting the Case for Meditation in Primary and Secondary Schools.* Available from 14 Carroll House, Craven Terrace, London W2 3PP.

Levey, J. (1987) *The Fine Arts of Relaxation, Concentration and Meditation: Ancient Skills for Modern Minds*. London: Wisdom Publications.

Mann, John (1999) *Moment of Christ*. London: Medio Media.

McDonald, Kathleen (1984) *How to Meditate: A Practical Guide*. Boston: Wisdom Publications.

Miller, J. P. (1994) *The Contemplative Practitioner: Meditation in Education and the Professions*. London: Beign and Garvey.

Murdock, M. (1987) *Spinning Inward*. Boston: Shambhala.

Nash, W. (1992) *People Need Stillness*. London: Darton, Longman & Todd.

Robb, J. and Letts, H. (1995) *Creating Kids Who Can*. London: Hodder & Stoughton.

Rozen, D. (1994) *Meditating with Children: The Art of Concentration and Centering*. Planetary Publications, PO Box 66, Boulder Creek, Calif. 95006 USA, tel: 408 338 2161.

Rozen, D. (n.d.) *Meditating with Children*. Tape for pre-school children and upwards, Planetary Publications, PO Box 66, Boulder Creek, Calif. 95006, USA, tel: 408 338 2161.

Scott, A. (ed.) (1989) *Insight*. Taunton, Somerset: Somerset County Council.

Sharron, H. (1994) *Changing Children's Minds*. Birmingham: Sharron Publishing.

Sherwood, C. (1995) *Making Friends with Ourselves*. Bath: Kidsmed.

Smith, P. and Smith, G. (1989) *Meditation: A Treasury of Technique*. Saffron Walden: C. W. Daniel.

Stewart, Mary and McCarthy Philips, Mary (1992) *Yoga for Children*. London: Vermilion (Ebury Press).

Stone, M. (1995) *Don't Just Do Something, Sit There*. Norwich: Religious and Moral Education Press.

Wood, E. (1949) *Concentration: An Approach to Meditation*. New York: Quest Books (available through Watkins Books).

Wood, E. (n.d.) *(Losing It Is*. Video documentary about the elusive zone, a state of heightened awareness/performance resulting from concentrated stillness and meditation. Available from Union Pictures, 36 Marshall Street, London W1V 1LL, tel: 0207 287 5110.

2. Buddhism and Buddhist Meditation

Batchelor, S. (1998) *Buddhism Without Belief: A Contemporary Guide to Awakening*. London: Bloomsbury.

Carrithers, M. (1983) *The Buddha*. Oxford: Oxford University Press.

Chah, Ajahn (1975) *A Still Forest Pool*, Kornfield and Breitner (eds.). New York: Quest.

Dalai Lama (1996) *Kindness, Clarity and Insight*. New York: Snow Lion.

Khan Noor Inayat (1985) *Twenty Jataka Tales*. London: East-West Publications.

Khema, Ayya (1987) *Being Nobody, Going Nowhere*. London: Wisdom Publications.

Reps, P. (1982) *Zen Flesh, Zen Bones*. Harmondsworth: Penguin.

Seeing the Way: Buddhist Reflections on the Spiritual Life. An Anthology of Teachings by English-Speaking Disciples of Ajahn Chah. Hemel Hempstead: Amaravati Publications.

Sumedho, Ajahn (1987) *Mindfulness: The Path to the Deathless*. Hemel Hempstead: Amaravati Publications.

Sumedho, Ajahn (1992) *Cittaviveka: Teachings from the Silent Mind*. Hemel Hempstead: Amaravati Publications.

Thich Nhat Hanh (1984) *The Miracle of Mindfulness: A Manual on Meditation*. Berkeley: Paralax.

Thich Nhat Hanh (1985) *A Guide to Walking Meditation*. Berkeley: Paralax.

Thich Nhat Hanh (1993) *Present Moment, Wonderful Moment*. London: Rider.

Trungpa, Chogyam (1973) *Cutting Through Spiritual Materialism*. Berkeley, Calif.: Shambala.

Videos

Thich Nhat Hanh (n.d.) *A Guide to Walking Meditation*. London: Meridian Trust.

The Art of Meditation. London: Meridian Trust.

3. Christian Meditation

Books

Freeman, Laurence (1986) *Light Within*. Berkhamsted: Medio Media.

Freeman, Laurence (1992) *Christian Meditation: Your Daily Practice*. Berkhamsted: Medio Media.

Freeman, Laurence (1997) *Aspects of Love*. Berkhamsted: Medio Media.

Main, John (1982) *Letters from the Heart*. Berkhamsted: Medio Media.

Main, John (1987) *Word into Silence*. Berkhamsted: Medio Media.

Main, John (1997) *Awakening*. Berkhamsted: Medio Media.

Main, John (2000) *Christian Meditation: The Gethsemani Talks*. Berkhamsted: Medio Media.

O'Hea, Eileen (1997) *Woman: Her Intuition for Otherness*. Berkhamsted: Medio Media.

O'Hea, Eileen (1997) *Silent Wisdom, Hidden Light: On Retreat with Eileen O'Hea*. Berkhamsted: Medio Media.

Video

Freeman, Lawrence (n.d.). *Coming Home* Tucson, Arizona: Medio Media.

Audio Tapes

Freeman, Laurence *All and Nothing*. (6 tapes of 60 minutes).

Main, John *Christian Meditation: The Essential Teaching*. (3 tapes of 90 minutes).

Main, John *In the Beginning*. (6 tapes of 60 minutes).

All the above are available from and published by: Medio Media, The World Community for Christian Meditation, 23 Kensington Square, London W8 5HN, tel. & fax: 020 8440 7769. e-mail: *LondonCentre@wccm.freeserve.co.uk*. web-site: *http://www.mediomedia.com*.

de Mello, Anthony (1984) *The Song of the Bird*. New York: Image Doubleday.

4. Christian Meditation with Children
Reehorst, Jane (1986) *Guided Meditations for Children 1*. Iowa: Wm. C. Brown.
Reehorst, Jane (1991) *Guided Meditations for Children 2*. Iowa: Wm. C. Brown. These books give a wide selection of meditation scripts based on Bible stories. Although they are very confessional in their approach they are easily adapted.
Simon, Madeleine (1993) *Born Contemplative*. London: Darton, Longman & Todd, only available from Medio Media (see address above).
von Wezeman, Phyllis and Fournier, Jude Dennis (1996) *20 Prayer Lessons for Children*. Mystic, Conn.: Twenty-Third Publications. This book provides a variety of active ideas for responses to meditation. It is confessional but easily adapted.

5. Krishnamurti and Meditation
Krishnamurti, J. (1955) *Education and the Significance of Life*. London, Gollancz.
Krishnamurti, J. (1973) *The Only Revolution*. Mary Lutyens (ed.), London: Gollancz.
Krishnamurti, J. (1982) *Krishnamurti's Journal*. New York: Harper-SanFrancisco.
Krishnamurti, J. (1996) *Questioning Krishnamurti: J. Krishnamurti in Dialogue*. London: Thorsens.
    The writings of Krishnamurti and audiotapes and videos of his talks are available from: The Krishnamurti Foundation Trust, Brockwood Park, Bramdean, Hampshire, SO24 0LQ, UK, tel: 01962 771525, fax: 01962 771159, e-mail: *info@brockwood.org.uk*.

6. Psychology and Meditation
Csikszentmihalyi, M. (1990) *Flow: The Psychology of Optimal Experience*. New York: Harper & Row.
Goleman, D. (1989) *The Meditative Mind*. Los Angeles: J. P. Tarcher.
Maslow, A. (1962) *Towards a Psychology of Being*. New York: Van Nostrand Reinhold.
Murphy, M. and Donovan, S. (1997) *The Physical and Psychological Effects of Meditation*. Sausalito, Calif.: Institute of Noetic Sciences.
West, M. (ed.) (1987) *The Psychology of Meditation*. Oxford: Clarendon Press.

7. Circle Time
Mosely, Jenny (1996) *Quality Circle Time in the Primary Classroom*. Wisbech: LDA.
Mosely, Jenny (1999) *Quality Circle Time in the Secondary School*. Wisbech: LDA.
Mosely, Jenny (1999) *More Quality Circle Time*. Wisbech: LDA.

8. Publications on Education and Students' Learning
Bettelheim, B. (1991) *The Uses of Enchantment: The Meaning and Importance of Fairy Tales*. London: Penguin.
Blagg, N. (1991) *Can We Teach Intelligence?* Hillside, New Jersey: Laurence Erlbaum.

Claxton, G. (1999) *Wise Up: The Challenge of Lifelong Learning*. London: Bloomsbury.

Cooling, Margaret (1990) *Assemblies for Primary Schools*. ACT (Association of Christian Teachers) and Norwich, RMEP (Religious and Moral Education Press).

DFEE (1994) *Circular 1/94*. London: HMSO.

Dryden, Gordon and Vos, Jeanette (1994) *The Learning Revolution*. Aylesbury, Bucks: Accelerated Learning Systems.

Erricker, C. (1998) Spiritual confusion: a critique of current educational policy in England and Wales. *International Journal of Children's Spirituality*, **3**(1), 51–64.

Erricker, C., Erricker, J., Ota, C., Sullivan, D., and Fletcher, M. (1997) *The Education of the Whole Child*. London: Cassell.

Fisher, R. (1990) *Teaching Children to Think*. Hemel Hempstead: Simon & Schuster.

Gardner, H. (1983) *Frames of Mind: A Theory of Multiple Intelligences*. New York: Basic Books.

Goleman, D. (1995) *Emotional Intelligence*. New York: Bantam Books.

Greenfield, S. (1995) *Journey to the Centre of the Mind*. New York: W. H. Freeman.

Greenfield, S. (1997) *The Human Brain: A Guided Tour*. London: Weidenfeld & Nicolson.

Hammond, J., Hay, D., Moxon, J., Netto, B., Raban, K., Straugheir, G. and Williams, C. (1990) *New Methods in Religious Education: An Experiential Approach*. London: Oliver and Boyd/Longman.

International Journal of Children's Spirituality. Abingdon: Carfax.

Jenson, E. (1994) *The Learning Brain*. San Diego, Calif.: Turning Point.

Lipman, M. (1988) *Philosophy Goes to School*. Philadelphia: Temple University Press.

Lipman, M. (1991) *Thinking in Education*. Cambridge: Cambridge University Press.

McCarthy, K. (2000) *Messier than the Models: Spirituality at the Chalkface*. Oxford: Farmington Institute for Christian Studies.

Meek, M., Warlow, A., Barton, G. (eds.) (1977) *The Cool Web: The Pattern of Children's Reading*. London: The Bodley Head.

National Curriculum Council (1993) *Spiritual and Moral Development: A Discussion Paper*. York: NCC.

Nixon, Jon, Martin, Jane, McKeowan, Penny and Ranson, Stewart (1996) *Encouraging Learning: Towards a Theory of the Learning School*. Buckingham: Open University Press.

Ravens, J. C. (1965) *The Guide to the Standard Progressive Matrices*. London: H. K. Lewis.

Rose, C. (1985) *Accelerated Learning*. Aylesbury, Bucks: Accelerated Learning Systems Ltd.

SCAA (1994) *Model Syllabuses for Religious Education*. London: School Curriculum and Assessment Authority.

SCAA (1995) *Spiritual and Moral Development*, Discussion Paper No. 3, London: School Curriculum and Assessment Authority.

SCAA (1996) *Discussion Paper 6. Education for Adult Life: The Spiritual and Moral Development of Young People*. London: SCAA.

Shute, C. (1998) *Edmond Holmes and 'The Tragedy of Education'*, Nottingham: Educational Heretics Press.

9. Further and Wider Reading

Abhishiktananda, A. (1974) *Saccidannanda: A Christian Approach to Advaitic Experience*. Delhi: S.P.C.K.

Allison, Dorothy (1996) *Two or Three Things I Know for Sure*. New York: Plume.

Dodd, C. H. (1978) *The Meaning of Paul for Today*. London: Fount.

Eliade, M. (1997) *From Primitives to Zen*. London: Fount.

Frith, N. (1976) *The Legend of Krishna*. London: Abacus.

Hunt, Marsha (ed.) (1999) *The Junk Yard: Voices from an Irish Prison*. Edinburgh: Mainstream Publishing.

Manheimer, R. J. (1977) *Kierkegaard as Educator*. Berkeley: University of California Press.

10. Further Useful Addresses

Amaravati Buddhist Centre, Great Gaddesden, Hemel Hempstead, Herts. HP1 3BZ, UK. Amaravati publications are available for free distribution only, although a donation is welcomed. They produce a number of publications on Buddhist meditation, run a summer school for children, and produce a magazine for children, *Rainbows*.

ISKCON Educational Services, Bhaktivedanta Manor, Dharam Marg, Hilfield Lane, Aldenham, Watford, Herts. UK, WD2 8EZ. Tel: 01923 859578. ISKON supply books, posters and artefacts from the Hindu tradition and specialist input in schools and colleges.

SAPERE (Society for the Advancement of Philosophical Enquiry and Reflection in Education): contact Roger Sutcliffe, North Mead House, 3 North Mead, Puriton, Somerset TA7 8DD. Tel: 01278 683478, e-mail: *rogersutcliffe@orangenet.co.uk*. SAPERE provide courses for teachers.

Tantra Ltd., 48 Kensington Park Road, Bristol BS4 3HU. Tel: 0117 9724708, Fax: 0117 9724709, Web site: *http://www.tantra.co.uk*. Tantra Designs supply various posters and artefacts from the Buddhist and other eastern traditions.

Index